GHETTONATION

ALSO BY CORA DANIELS

Black Power Inc.

GHETTO**NATION**

Dispatches
from America's
Culture War

CORA DANIELS

BROADWAY BOOKS

New York

For my husband, Rondai,

who constantly overfills my highest expectations.

BROADWAY

Copyright © 2007 by Cora Daniels

All Rights Reserved

Published in the United States by Broadway Books, an imprint
of The Doubleday Publishing Group, a division
of Random House, Inc., New York.
www.broadwaybooks.com

A hardcover edition of this book was originally published
in 2007 by Doubleday.

BROADWAY BOOKS and its logo, a letter B bisected on the
diagonal, are trademarks of Random House, Inc.

LIBRARY OF CONGRESS CATALOGING-IN-PUBLICATION DATA
Daniels, Cora.
    Ghettonation : dispatches from america's culture war /
by Cora Daniels. — 1st paperback ed.
        p. cm.
    Originally published: New York: Doubleday, c2007.
    Includes index.
    1. Inner cities—United States. 2. African Americans—Social
conditions. 3. Popular culture—United States. I. Title.

    HN59.2.D33 2008
    307.760973—dc22

                        2008012402

ISBN 978-0-7679-2240-1

PRINTED IN THE UNITED STATES OF AMERICA

10 9 8 7 6 5 4 3 2 1

FIRST PAPERBACK EDITION

ACKNOWLEDGMENTS

Reading books, for the most part, is a private and, if you're lucky, a "curl-up" indulgence But writing them, regardless of what we authors might fool ourselves into thinking, is really a community effort. This book would not be possible without a bunch of spectacular folks holding me up. Here are my shout-outs:

First I would like to thank Ghettonation. From where I'm from, to where I am, to where I hope to go, it is the pulse of the street that constantly inspires the best in me. I would like to give a special thanks to Bed-Stuy, Brooklyn, which I now call home. Thanks to the young folks on the corners, to the Mr. Pops on the stoops, the Mama-saids over the windowsills, and everyone surviving in between. Thank you for welcoming my reporter's notebook and the questions that always come with it. And thanks for teaching me something every day.

I would also like to give a heartfelt thanks to my editor, Clarence Haynes, who got it—all of it—from the beginning. Thank you for constantly challenging my work and thoughts and pushing me farther than I knew I could go. Thanks for all your never-ending support. Working with you was a gift. Also a big thanks to Doubleday and Janet Hill and her team at Harlem Moon, for embracing me and treating me like a member of a special family.

To my agent and friend Nicholas Roman Lewis, thanks for always thinking big and forcing me to think bigger. You have been a much-appreciated fan of *Ghettonation* even before a single word of it was written. Thank you for your faith.

Thank you to some of the big brains across academia and beyond whose work always makes me think. Some noteworthies would have to be the individualism of Todd Boyd, the intellect of Mary Pattillo, Jill Nelson's passion, Ellis Cose's eye, and my favorite anthropologists Deborah Thomas and John L. Jackson Jr. You influence me more than you know.

Thanks to the folks at *Fortune* for supporting my life as an author and generously giving me time off to write a book about worlds that initially might be seen as vastly different from those typically covered by the magazine.

Thank you to my circle. *Ghettonation* forced me to open up and look inside and expose my village. A serious thank-you to my friends and family and other close ones for allowing me to pick through my memories. Especially, thanks to Bruno Navarro, Donald Vick, Joyce Davis, Vanessa Lipske, Susan Chapman, Anthony Guinyard, Kimberly Allers, Lester Jackson, Shawn Baldwin, Roy Johnson, Amber Dominguez, Brian Dominguez, Ayanna Young, RK Byers, Duana Butler, Daniel Howard, Terrence Fisher, Alyce Lee, Terri Cade-Hill, Amanda Williams, Sheba Smith, Wendy Merritt, Ernie Suggs, Jennifer Parker, Tessi Roberts, Meta Mereday, Taylor Lindsey, Melissa Bahamond, Tamisha Kelly, and Michelle Patterson for your invaluable observations, insights, and experiences. These pages are our story and this book would not be possible without y'all.

To Uncle Bugs, Aunt Candy, Chub, and the rest of the Pittsburgh clan, thank you for filling my world with so much fun, laughter, and love.

To my mom, thank you for empowering me with your love and always believing I could do anything. Thanks to my brother, Omar, for a lifetime of friendship that I continue to lean on. And to my dad, not a day goes by that I don't wish I had one more with you; thanks for giving me so much to miss.

Most of all, thank you to my beloved husband Rondai, for all the little things as well as the big. Thank you for making me question, instead of tsk-tsking. Thank you for loving my ghetto side and my non. And thank you for your heartfelt support. Nothing means anything without you. And to Maya, my bundle of pure joy, thank you for making me care so much about how we are living. Thank you both for the journey.

To all my deepest gratitude.

CONTENTS

INTRODUCTION

ghet-to *n.* (*Merriam-Webster's Dictionary*) [Italian, from Venetian dialect *ghèto* island where Jews were forced to live, literally, foundry (located on the island), from *ghetàr* to cast, from Latin *jactare* to throw]
1: a quarter of a city in which Jews were formerly required to live
2: a quarter of a city in which members of a minority group live especially because of social, legal, or economic pressure
3a: an isolated group <a geriatric *ghetto*> **b:** a situation that resembles a ghetto especially in conferring inferior status or limiting opportunity <stuck in daytime TV's *ghetto*>[1]

ghet-to *adj.* [twenty-first-century everyday conversation]
1a: behavior that makes you want to say "Huh?"
b: actions that seem to go against basic home training and common sense
2: used to describe something with inferior status or

limited opportunity, usually used with so <That's so
ghetto. He's so *ghetto*.>

3: a quarter of a city in which members of a minority
group live, especially because of social, legal, or economic pressure

4: common misusage: authentic, Black, keepin' it
real

When was the last time you used, heard, thought, snickered, whispered (under your breath), shouted (at the radio), the word *ghetto*?

I use it so many times a day I can't even count. When the teenagers
sitting on milk crates outside my house in Brooklyn get rowdy playing
cards late on a school night. When the man-boys on the corner see
my wedding ring as just a challenge instead of something to respect.
Whenever I turn on BET, period. *Ghet-to*.

And it's not fabulous.

You say it, too. Admit it. I have a friend who stretches the word
out whenever he utters it, as if it needs any more emphasis: As in
gh-e-e-e-e-et——to-o-o-o-o-o-o.

I've spent more than three decades becoming an expert on ghetto,
both *ghet-to* and *gh-e-e-e-e-et——to-o-o-o-o-o-o*. My training? My life.
But it wasn't until recently, when those ghetto moments got overwhelming, that I felt compelled to write about it. The question most
authors hate to answer while they are still writing is the dreaded "What
is your book about?" Or maybe it's just me. As a journalist I'm much
more comfortable spreading the word about others than talking about
anything that I might be doing. It is more than the panicky "What do I
say?" flash of shyness. Instead, there is this initial wave of self-doubt and
fear that whoever you are talking to is going to give you that look. That
"what are you talking about?" look. Or the "why would I want to read
about that?" look. Or the worst, the "fading into total bored disinterest"
look that grows more pronounced with each of your sentences. When

you are still writing, looks like these can push you into an unproductive tailspin as you ask yourself, What *am* I talking about? Why *would* anyone want to read this?—and disinterest. It's hard to describe a work in progress because while you're writing you're still on the trail of discovery and development.

While writing *Ghettonation*, I never had to answer that "what is it about?" question. The moment people heard the title they assumed they knew intimately what I was writing on. Everyone, it seems, thinks they know ghetto. Even our great thinkers: academics. "Ghetto?" asks Dr. John L. Jackson Jr., a communication and anthropology professor at the University of Pennsylvania who has spent his career theorizing about race and class. "We know it almost immediately when we see it, when we hear it." No doubt, professor.

Still, I found it pretty remarkable that no one would let me even fumble my way through some awkward explanation of my project. Instead, just hearing *"ghetto"* usually sent them—strangers, close friends, folks on the corner, in the beauty parlor, on the stoop, at the office, on the subway, after work—into a tailspin. Reactions were tinged with a bit of anger, a bit of frustration, and a huge bout of "I just got to get this off my chest."

"Are you going to write about nails and gold teeth, about weaves— blond and red—about baby bottles filled with Pepsi, about babymamas . . . ?" people wanted to know.

"Yes . . . maybe . . . no . . . , and more," I wanted people to know.

Ghetto, you see, is a mind-set. And that is so much more.

As all-consuming as ghetto is in these days of gold teeth, weaves— blond and red—Pepsi-filled baby bottles, and babymamas, ghetto has a history. The original ghetto was in Venice. It was the Jewish quarter in this Catholic city. Before it became the Jewish area it was an iron foundry or *ghèto*, and thus the name was born. In the fourteenth century, gates surrounded the ghetto. Non-Jews were not allowed to live in the ghetto, and Jews were not allowed to leave it. The gates were locked at night. Besides the literal gates, the world's first ghetto was remarkable in another sense, too: it was an affluent neighborhood—home to Jewish merchants and moneylenders. By the seventeenth century, with the encouragement of the Vatican, ghettos spread across Italy. Each had its own justice system, further isolating these districts from papal rule. Then in the nineteenth century, driven by the equality ideals of the French Revolution, the walls of the ghetto came crashing down. Pope Pius IX had Europe's last ghetto—Rome's—destroyed, walls and system, in 1870.

During World War II the Jewish ghetto was resurrected by the Nazis. By 1940 it was being used as a stopover on the way to the concentration camps. The ghettos were overcrowded communities of filth, starvation, violence, and despair. The Warsaw ghetto in Poland housed close to 400,000 people in a 3.5-square-mile area that had previously been home to about 160,000 people. This time instead of just gates, the threat of being shot by armed guards ensured that Jews stayed in the ghetto.

The Jews of Europe who survived the Nazi horrors were freed in 1945. Meanwhile in America's cities, ghettos fed by housing discrimination, segregation laws, and racism were starting to flourish.* Just as ghettos were once a part of every major city in Italy, they were now in every major city in America. Instead of Jews, Black faces were the ones now trapped inside. Ghettos were overcrowded communities of filth, starvation (maybe not for food but for hope), violence, and despair. Instead of gates, highways often artificially divided and isolated these neighborhoods from the rest of the city, helping to keep folks in. And the threat of being shot or stabbed or beaten by armed natives guaranteed that others stayed out of the ghetto.[2]

---

* About the same time, under the apartheid regime in South Africa, Soweto was being created specifically as a place for Black Africans to live, ushered by law out of more desirable areas of Johannesburg. Today, in this post-apartheid era, Soweto is still billed by South Africa's tourism industry as the must-see "ghetto" for anyone's vacation.

Coming full circle, ghettos have traveled back to Europe. Today in France when people talk about ghettos, they are referring to high-rise public housing complexes built far away from the city centers to house African and Arab Muslim immigrants. The overcrowded communities of filth, starvation (for a voice), violence, and despair are hotbeds for Islamic fundamentalists on the prowl for their next terrorist recruits.[3] The alternative justice system that has sprung up in France is reminiscent of the way gangs can rule the streets of America's ghettos.

That's the history. Sometime after the Jewish slums of the Nazi era and the urban slums of America, after the dream was deferred, ghetto stopped being just a place on the map and became also a place of mind. Now ghetto no longer refers to where you live; it is *how* you live. It is a mind-set.

That is why the word slips from our lips so often. (How did we ever talk about people without it before?) The jump from an impoverished physical landscape to an impoverished mental one is harder to trace than is the history of the word itself. Honestly, I am not exactly sure when the transformation happened. It was such a natural and gradual shift. But for anyone who is listening, there is no denying that these days *ghetto*, as it is used, has indeed made that leap. I did not reposition *ghetto* from noun to adjective—we all did that. As a journalist I am merely shining a spotlight on how we are living. As an author I am compelled to explore, theorize, and most of all challenge what post-leap ghetto means for each of us and for all of us. And as a Black woman surviving, and drowning, in Ghettonation, I am defining ghetto as a mind-set.

A mind-set that thinks it is acceptable to be playing cards on the street to all hours on a school night instead of doing homework. A mind-set that thinks the *M* words—monogamy and marriage—are bad language. A mind-set that thinks it is fine to bounce, baby, bounce in some video, as if that makes it any different from performing such a display on a table, on a pole, on some john's lap, or on the corner. And a mind-set that thinks a record deal and a phat beat in the background makes it okay to say . . . to say—well, I *do* know what bad language is, so I won't say. Most of all, ghetto is a mind-set that embraces the worst. It is the embodiment of expectations that have gotten dangerously too low.

Granted, to now use *ghetto* to define such an undesirable mind-set, given the word's long association with poverty, could be seen as another way for people with middle-class sensibilities to demonize the poor. There is no doubt in my mind that such classism did contribute to ghetto making the leap from place to being. It was disgust for the ghetto that led to using the word to describe behavior that also inspired disgust. But I would argue that a mind-set has no class boundaries. And I have no problem with labeling folks from *every* rung of the ladder as ghetto.

After Jamie Foxx won his historic best actor Oscar for *Ray*, he did the obligatory rounds of late-night and morning talk shows to get his applause. When Jay Leno asked the Oscar winner what he had done after the Academy Awards to celebrate, the former *Booty Call* star recapped his party appearances, broke into the mandatory seated dance move performed by Black guests on white shows, and proudly declared: "Ya know, we kept it ghetto." An unfazed Leno nodded. He seemed to know exactly what keeping it ghetto meant.

Feel that? The worlds just collided. Welcome to Ghettonation.

The most obvious reason for this brave new world is the pop culturalization of ghetto, from music to movies to TV to sports. Hip-hop exploded when it embraced ghetto, and it has seeped into every nook and cranny of American life. Even JCPenney, which holds a disturbing place in most people's memories for showcasing that all-American tradition of polyester pant suits, featured commercials showcasing eight-year-old all-American white kids break-dancing to "Baby Got Back" to sell *back*packs during the chain's *back* to school campaign. (Why is this ghetto? Because now there are eight-year-olds going around singing "Baby Got Back" as if it were the "Wheels on the Bus.")

When my husband and I travel abroad, whether it be to South America, Europe, or the Caribbean, at some point during the trip he will be asked, nicely, respectfully, and with no ill intent, if he is a rapper. How else would a young Black man have cash to spend? The first couple of times I could not hold back my fits of laughter as I imagined my husband, the doctor, spitting rhymes to his patients in the OR before operating on their eyes. (Yes, young Black eye surgeons do exist!) Now we've learned to milk the stereotypes for any perks we can get. In Mexico we used our Blackness to enjoy the pool of an expensive resort where we were not even guests after we discovered that the hotel was overrun with a group of NFL players staying there. (Yes, we be ghetto.) My husband is only five-foot-nine and a buck-sixty on a good day, and I, always coated in newsprint from my pile of newspapers and maps that I insist on for poolside entertainment, am far from a trophy wife, but none of the hotel staff ever questioned that we were not "with the team," giving us the same special treatment as all the other Black NFL bodies at the resort. Even in Morocco they called my husband Puff Daddy and wanted to buy his "hip-hop" sunglasses right off his face, constantly gave us insider tours, and slipped us free food and mint tea, in marked contrast to the lack of hospitality shown the other American tourists we came across. And because of that constant connection, all of us being seen as one, sometimes the resentment and frustration over ghetto ways can be even more visceral. *Why we gotta be like that?*

With that first crossover *yo*, my generation of post–civil rights babies has had to put up with ghetto as mainstream. At the office we can hear: "Yo, Snoop is sweeeeet, see him on MTV last night?" (Unfortunately, these exact words have been thrown my way at the office . . . by a superior.) Coming of age in this ghetto mainstream means we can speak the language, can sport the style, know the references—we just can no longer tolerate it anymore.

I set out to examine how we are living and discovered how ghetto became chic—for all of us. Martha Stewart helped convince me of this. It was her first Thanksgiving as an ex-con and she had Patti LaBelle on her cooking show. The domestic diva and the Grammy-winning singer were trying to whip up some "Screamin' Mean Greens" from LaBelle's grandmama's recipe. In her designer finest and perfectly coifed, Patti turned to Martha and informed her that steam wasn't a friend of the sistas. "I'm tryin' to stay cute," Patti said, trying to protect her flip-do amid the steam. Martha protested that the steam wasn't a good friend of white girls, either. "Martha, you couldn't be ghetto if you tried," the singer chastised the host as the two stood in the ultimate all-American kitchen. To which Martha—queen of all that is proper—Stewart, shot back: "Oh, I can get ghetto when I need to."

That is the thing with a mind-set. It is not limited to a class or a race. Some things are worth repeating: ghetto is *not* limited to a class or a race. Ghetto is found in the heart of the nation's inner cities as well as in the heart of the nation's most cherished suburbs; among those too young to understand (we hope) and those old enough to know better; in little white houses all the way to the White House; in corporate corridors, Ivy League havens, and, of course, in Hollywood. More devastating, ghetto is also packaged and sold in the form of music, TV, books, fashion, and movies and then sold around the world. Bling, bling—which, by the way, was added to the *Oxford English Dictionary* back in 2003. (Ghetto.) Bottom line, ghetto is contagious, and no one is immune no matter how much we like to suck our teeth and shake our heads at what we think is happening only someplace else.

I can remember the instant I knew I had to write this book. It was the moment that Paris Hilton made me think. It was the first season of *The Simple Life*. Not ever having consciously associated the hotel chain with a family surname, I had never even heard of the blindingly blond bimbo before. Suddenly, with a sex tape under her belt and a reality show to launch her no-talent, she was everywhere. For the first season the show sent Paris and rich girl gal pal Nicole Richie (Lionel's daughter) to live as far, far away from Beverly Hills, credit cards, Rodeo Drive, sushi, and nightlife as Hollywood could think of: a farm in Arkansas. The exaggerated fish-out-of-water setup was good for some mindless laughs. One day I was watching *The Simple Life*, mesmerized by the outrageous antics of Lionel's brat, Nicole, as she cursed out unsuspecting cows *(Hello?)* when Paris finally did something that stopped me in my tracks. The multimillionaire heiress was trying to start the old pickup truck that belonged to her host family. In between giggles (as much a staple of the show as the designer outfits, bottle tans, and the I-wish-I-hadn't-seen-it Paris crack), she could not get the truck's rusty engine to kick over. Frustrated, Paris squealed, "This truck is so ghetto." That was the moment.

Paris, the oldest of four Hilton kids, was raised in a suite in the Waldorf-Astoria Hotel in Manhattan with stints at the $10-million family mansion in Bel Air and summers in the Hamptons. Her inheritance is estimated by *Forbes* magazine to be about $50 million, and she reportedly makes more than $6 million a year from appearances, modeling, and movies. Her world is as far from most people's reality as it can get. Yet, of all people, Paris Hilton utters on national TV that something "is ghetto"? How would she know? What could she possibly mean by that?

I heard Paris say *ghetto* as I was sitting in my home in Bed-Stuy, Brooklyn, where sometimes I have to struggle to hear the TV over the constant bounce-your-head beat, *pssssst* of the corner, mamas cursing at their babies, and even the occasional gunshot outside my door. It was that moment that I realized that ghetto was something larger than I thought. Mind-sets usually are.

...

Ghettonation is the story of the mind-set. Chapter 1, "Livin' Large," explores what this world is like up close and personal. Because ghetto has become so rampant, it also runs the danger of becoming mundane, so sometimes we all need to be reminded to open our eyes and see it.

Chapter 2, "Exporting Dirty Laundry," follows the money. The bottom line is that while ghetto is costing us more than can be put into words, it is also making corporate America's richest companies richer.

Chapter 3, "Ghettonation Speaks": Enough with the discussions from high places about what we are sure the problem is. Hear from the young and folks around the way themselves, in their own words.

Chapter 4, "Please, Baby, Please," honestly examines our relationships while . . . chapter 5, "Family Values," sees what these relationships mean for families.

Chapter 6, "Nigga What, Nigga Who," listens to the words that are coming out of our mouths.* I heard Ice Cube boasting on TV recently that he didn't mind if someone called him Nigger, or rather, he didn't mind being called Nigga, just don't call him Bitch.[4] What are we saying nowadays? Language is the ticket to opening doors. It allows us to reach off-limit worlds as well as limiting worlds. Foreign lands don't have to be beyond these borders; they can be within them. There is lawyerspeak, doctorspeak, academicspeak, reporterspeak, and ghettospeak. The goal has always been to be as fluent in as many languages as possible. That is changing. Ghettospeak is now not just people's first language, but their last. And it is isolating a community.

Chapter 7, "School Me," discusses education and the dangers of low expectations.

Chapter 8, "Cos Speaks," tries to dissect the storm created when Papa Huxtable gave us all a spanking.

Chapter 9, "Do You Speak?" is a call to action. Ghetto will continue to spread as long as we stay silent.

---

* Thank you, Chris Tucker.

■ ■ ■

To discover how we live, I started by actually talking to young folks in our communities. Teenagers in my Bed-Stuy neighborhood, teenagers in Atlanta, D.C., suburban Long Island, California, Pittsburgh, Chicago, Cleveland, the West Coast, East Coast, North, and South, wherever I could find a corner. On the train I took notes as I eavesdropped. I hung out at high schools and Internet cafés where the teenage universe is enlarged by chat rooms and online games played in cyberspace. Some things are definitely different. For instance, I learned the game of choice these days among young people at those cybercafés is called Guns. Really. But some things sounded familiar. Namely, they are worried, too. I heard the "things are getting bad" refrain, a lot.

I also discovered that everyone thinks wherever they are from has the lockdown on ghetto. In some kind of warped hometown loyalty, sometime during the conversation folks would stake their claim to owning the bottom. Philly is more ghetto than D.C. Or is it that D.C. is more ghetto than Philly? Or Dallas (L.A.) is more ghetto than L.A. (Dallas). Chicago (Detroit) is more ghetto than Detroit (Chicago). Richmond (St. Louis) is more ghetto than St. Louis (Richmond). Small towns are ghetto, too: big up to Poughkeepsie, New York, and Asbury Park, New Jersey. So are the suburbs: Brentwood in Long Island, New York, and Lithonia in DeKalb County, Georgia, are in the house. And don't forget the rural areas, one e-mail from a North Carolina country boy begged me. Augusta, Georgia; Cadiz, Kentucky; Eatonville, Florida, are keepin' it real. I caught myself falling for the trap one day when talking to Vanessa, who hails from the ATL. Atlanta is more ghetto than Brooklyn, she assured me. My instinct was to protest. Then she reminded me, "We gave birth to Crunk!" Well, she does have a point. Jokes aside, this isn't really a contest anyone wants to win. Or they shouldn't want to. The fact that it isn't just Brooklyn, my block, my neighborhood, my city, my state, doesn't give me much comfort. It means ghetto is everywhere. That's the problem with a mind-set.

And that is something we shouldn't want, either. The consequences of ghetto are no joke: it is destroying us.

I started conversations with the young and the folks around my way because too many of us like to talk about, like to tsk-tsk, like to shake our heads in Cosby indignation, like to suck our teeth and whisper under our breath about how ghetto it all is without actually ever talking with the people we are tsk-tsking about. Now, let's be honest, what could be more ghetto than that?

Welcome to Ghettonation. Let the journey begin. . . .

PROLOGUE: I AM GHETTO

I am ghetto. The running joke among my friends is
that the only stuff to drink in my fridge is a Crayola-
bright color and comes in two-liter bottles. Movies
to me are BYOF (as in Bring Your Own Food) experiences. C'mon, what could be better than having some Popeye's chicken, a glass of orange soda,
and a twenty-five-cent bag of Cheez Doodles while
watching an overpriced movie? You know you'd
like some, too. I am ghetto because I'd rather sit on
my front stoop than in my backyard. And I consider
a plastic shopping bag an acceptable carryall.

I am not ghetto. I have a husband instead of babydaddies. I drive a
car that is completely paid off but so nondescript that even I forget what
it looks like sometimes. And when I drive and listen to music, I can still
hear the passengers speaking in the backseat. I also own only one pair
of sneakers, which I allow to get dirty.

I grew up in a too-small apartment in Lower Manhattan. I'll spare
you the clichés of the gritty streets, drugs, and trouble, because as has
happened to most gritty streets in New York City, gentrification has
taken the grit out, so the neighborhood I grew up in no longer exists.
Even back then there were grittier streets than mine, but, for the histor-

ical record: in one of those tenement walk-ups—before ghetto became fabulous—I shared a bunk bed with my younger brother until the day I went off to college. You had to walk through our room to get to the small apartment's only bathroom, making privacy a lifelong quest for all of us. Summers were so hot in that little bedroom with its ghetto heat (the uncomfortable combination of no ventilation and old radiators permanently stuck on full blast) that I am convinced that is why, still, I start to shiver if the temperature dips below ninety degrees. I know what it is like to go grocery shopping with food stamps and pennies. I am from a world where government cheese was considered a staple and Velveeta was what you hoped for. Yeah, that's ghetto. I can still remember watching my father add salt to everything from McDonald's french fries to watermelon since any food is better with just a little salt. This is where I am from. It is not who I am.

Before I realized I was a writer, I thought I'd be an architect. I even went to a special engineering high school with this dream in mind. I picked this dream not for any great understanding of building design but because of my admiration for a TV show. Mr. Brady on *The Brady Bunch* was an architect and could afford to take care of six kids, a dog, his lovely lady, *and* a maid. Not a bad life for someone who draws with a ruler. I wanted to be an architect, too. When I got to high school, though, and kept getting Cs in my drafting classes because I didn't have a proper desk at home big enough for my T-square drawings, my Mr. Brady dreams died quickly. The fact that I was taking career clues from the fantasy world of a moronic sitcom—*The Brady Bunch?!*—instead of the real world around me means, well, I am ghetto. But the dream is early proof that my mind always thought beyond my blocks. I am not ghetto.

I discovered I was ghetto when I got to college. (Imagine my Cheez Doodle–lovin' self at an Ivy League campus.) I accepted that I was ghetto when I went to grad school. I embraced that I was ghetto when I started working. (Where I come from is how I survive where I am; it reminds me that things could be worse.) And realized I was not ghetto when I returned back home.

Now, in keeping-it-real tradition, I live in gritty city streets, this time in Brooklyn, much like the streets I grew up in. But I feel like a straddler—both an insider and an outsider, comfortable and not. The ghetto choices around me, from talking trash too loud on the subway to choosing TV over books or snacking on KFC biscuits over anything else, make sense because I've been faced with those choices before. It is the (lack of) reasoning when it comes to making choices that does not make sense to me now. So I can see the kids on the corner and know, because I did it, too, why they stand there: the corner is the center of the world, even for the smallest ones. Still, I don't understand anymore why they would *want* to.

The tug between the why and the want is what I think about as I go about my daily routine. I admit it, even with my straddler vision, I don't always get the why. Why, for instance, does the cashier at my local grocery store insist on keeping her intricately painted, acrylic-enhanced nails so obscenely long that she needs a pencil to press the keys of her register and do her job? (I am not ghetto.) But I can't ignore what I don't understand . . . anymore.

I am a New Yorker so the subway is part of my routine. It is uniquely New York, and that is primarily the reason that I like it. But regardless of my hometown biases—big up to Brooklyn (I am ghetto!)—as a journalist I have to love the subway because it is a reflection of *how* we are. How we live, how we interact (or not), how we think. Unlike commuter trains, which shuttle like-minded suburbanites into the city, depositing them at the same predictable spot at the same predictable moment, or the rush-hour jammed freeways where cars safely isolate the familiar and repel the different, the subway is a true petri dish of Ghettonation because it snakes slowly through neighborhoods, placing extremes side by side and mixing natives who normally don't mix. If the explorers of yesterday wanted to discover new worlds today, they'd get on a subway instead of a boat. So to take a trip into Ghettonation, we start with the subway. These are my ghetto journeys.

Every morning on my way to the subway, no matter how early I leave for work, I pass the "knuckleheads on the corner." They are all dressed in the accepted uniform of the corner—perfectly color-coordinated baggy ensembles of mostly jeans and jerseys, blinding bling bling—platinum chains, diamond studs, oversized crosses—and sneakers, always. The dress code includes just enough sports colors to chest-thumpingly shout, "I'm a man, son," yet just enough sports colors to indicate that the memorabilia has nothing to do with the teams but, well, da colors. I am dressed in my best ghetto protective armor: work clothes. Sometimes it succeeds; most times it doesn't.

I am not ghetto.

There are thousands of corners like this in my neighborhood, my city, our country. The dedication that the manboys have to the corner is more than mine could ever be to the office. There is not a doubt in my mind that even on the days when I don't manage to roll out of bed for work, the corner is still manned.

Like some kind of 1950s sitcom, the knuckleheads wish me off to work each morning and welcome me home in the evening. Every day. Instead of a kiss, have-a-nice-day chatter, and the paper to start my day, the knuckleheads offer a *pssst*, baby-baby-please talk, and (little pieces of) paper. (For the digits, of course.)

As in "Pssssst, Mommmmmmi, God bless your smile. You're beautiful, you know that? What's your name, baby? C'mon, you can tell me your name. I just want to be friends. You think we can be friends? Here's my number. You gonna call me? Please, baby, baby, please."

And our journey has begun. As the straddler I can (and will) interpret this morning banter for those who need line-by-line translation. For now be thankful for the wait.

My journey continues. On the train, I see . . .

Young mothers with kids hanging off their arms like accessories. Sometimes on the weekends when I ride the train home late at night I stare at the young women with kids on the train at that hour and think how these women have been able to preserve their lives exactly as they were before they had children. The *New York Times*, the nation's paper of record, even ran a story once about miniskirt etiquette—basically how to maneuver the city streets in short, short skirts without exposure. The women weighing in on this unweighty issue were a perfect mosaic of the diversity of the nation. I see Black women, white women, Asian women, Latinas, young women, old women, big women, small women, hot women, leave-me-alone women, women who love women, women who love men, hardworking women, working-hard-at-not-working women, women who are mothers, women who are only daughters, girls masquerading as women, and women masquerading as girls. Just women. The picture used to illustrate the *Times* story was a three-panel step-by-step photo sequence of a mother—leaning on her baby's stroller—demonstrating the "move" she uses to sit on the subway without showing too much. I can't remember her face from the photo but I have seen *her* on the subway. There are lots of women like her. Despite the article's best attempts to spread its tsk-tsk morals about scantily clad women, I was more concerned about the tool used for the move: the baby stroller. I couldn't stop tsk-tsking about that baby-stroller-as-accessory to the rising hemline, and how now the stroller had become necessary for leverage to pull off the no-show move. Lives should change after you have children. Shouldn't they?

I am not ghetto.

On the train I see teenagers showboating the way teenagers do. The language has changed over the years from *brother* to *nigger* and from *sister* to *bitch*. These days that loud immature talk wouldn't make it past the FCC censors for foul language. *Fuck*, it seems, has replaced *the* as the most common word used in the English language. The words are so harsh and the sentences even harsher, that such talk cuts through the air, assaulting everyone's ears. I see adults on the train squirm and shake their heads. A few dare to stop hiding behind their newspapers for a moment to shoot dirty looks at the young people. But no one speaks. No one tells these kids to curb their tongues. Who is more ghetto, then—the teenagers who don't know any better or the rest of us who do and say nothing? Hiding myself, I look at these kids and remember the overstuffed knapsack I used to carry to school every day and wonder where their books are.

I see grown men playing video games, sleeping, staring blankly, or just plain relaxing as if the subway were their living room. Theirs is a carefreeness that can only come from still living under their mother's roof.

As the train passes through gentrified regions, the complexions get lighter but the scenes are remarkably similar. Ghetto unites. The young mothers from the beginning of my journey are replaced with older late-thirtysomething mothers (delayed by careers), with kids hanging off their arms like accessories.

Young women on their way to respectable office jobs wear stylish short, short skirts that blur the lines between work and play. I do it, too. I am ghetto. They paint their faces with little makeup mirrors and talk to their friends too loudly without respect for the subway car's shared airwaves. One could ask, where are their books, too?

Young twentysomethings, even thirtysomethings, recount their expensive weekends of clubs, alcohol, sex, alcohol, bars, alcohol, partying, alcohol. It is the kind of mock-adulthood carefreeness that comes from living in apartments they can afford only with their parents' help.

At each stop I see new groups of teenagers as every neighborhood adds its own legacy. If these teenage groups are separated by the race of their neighborhood, they are united by everything else. Which means everyone looks and sounds like they've jumped straight out of a BET video. The Black kids say things like "Ya know what I'm sayin'." Ditto say the Latinos. Ditto say the Italian kids. And the Asian kids. And the Jewish kids. And the WASPs say it, too. It seems that while the rest of us were hiding behind our newspapers, not saying a word, the knuckleheads on the corner became the most imitated role models in the nation. When the teenage talk gets too loud, some business-suit-clad commuters move to the next car. It is a temporary solution, but (white) flight always is.

It reminds me that the suburbs are just as ghetto.

Along cul-de-sacs and "lanes" and "roads" and manicured "drives" I see SUVs as big as military tanks; when archaeologists in the future dig up the remains of our civilization, they might wonder if we were constantly at war.

In parking lots instead of on corners young folks hang out into the wee hours of the morning. I see groups of white teenagers from nice neighborhoods, with safe schools and nice homes in bedroom communities, boasting about turning down elaborate family vacations and summer programs so they can drink cheap beer under the glow of the lights of the deserted parking lot. They stand guard and watch the road, making comments to those who enter the way the knuckleheads on my corner do.

"Straight chillin', man, this is what we do basically every night," says Matt, a seventeen-year-old from Wantagh, Long Island, one of those nice bedroom communities. A sixteen-year-old girl named Alicia, wearing a tiny T-shirt bearing the message COWGIRLS HAVE IT. COWBOYS WANT IT stretched tight across her breasts, shows off her new tongue piercing. She was going to get the connective tissue underneath the tongue done instead—web pierced—but she thinks guys like the studs on tongues better for, "you know."[1]

I see young professional couples already on their second marriages running from the distractions of the city to the 'burbs, determined to make these vows stick. The media called the phenomenon of these first marriages that tended to last less than five years and usually didn't produce kids "starter marriages." Is there anything more ghetto than to have a name for our relationship immaturity?

I see a real estate agent on a national home-decorating show complain that a particular house, in a typical suburban development, will not sell because it is void of "bling." "This house has no bling," she tells the defeated homeowner. The job for the team of makeover experts is to give it some "bling."

I hear men off to work in suits and swinging briefcases trying to slip into their chitchat a little "keeping it real" flavor—a misplaced *chillin'* here, a *bro* there—whatever the word of the moment was a few years back that they've picked up from ESPN, all to prove that they are still hip. Of course, it doesn't make them hip, but it does prove once again the power of ghetto vernacular.

And a cheap swipe but still true, I see malls—overflowing with people and lots of straps (thong and bra)—as cultural centers, town halls, and de facto baby-sitters.

I get off the subway in Midtown—at Rockefeller Center with its skyscrapers, shiny lobbies, skating rink, and bright lights. It is far, far away from my gritty streets in Brooklyn where my journey began. Passing a newsstand, I notice the *People* magazine headline announces that actress Gwyneth Paltrow is now a mother. Her daughter's name is Apple. (It reminded me of India, not the country, the name of my cousin. Actually it is Indya, since *y*'s are always better than *i*'s in Ghettonation.) So Gwyneth names her child Apple because the word is beautiful, the mother in her says, just as other mothers saw Asia, Diamond, Peaches, Tiffany (for the store, like Trump's daughter), and Indya.

My own middle name is pronounced *Yvonne* but has a spelling all its own. My husband's name was picked out of an African name book, but the first letter was then changed to an R because both his parents' names begin with an R too. It means spelling and pronunciation are mismatched, big-time. And I have a cousin who is named after his dad's favorite drink, E&J. Still, the unusual choice of naming a child after a fruit made me think, What is in a name, anyway? Could I be a victim of my own conservative snobbery not to see the beauty in Apple or Indya, too? Professors from MIT and the University of Chicago wanted to see what was in a name, too. They answered thousands of real newspaper want ads sending in identical résumés except for the name. One batch of résumés was sent with names like Kristen, Susan, and Brad. The other batch of the same résumés was sent to the same companies with names like Latoya, Shamika, and LaShawn. Guess what? The Brads and Kristens were 50 percent more likely to get called back for an interview than the Shamikas and LaShawns with the exact same résumés. Apparently there is a lot in a name. The researchers thought with the results of their LaShawn and Shamika résumés they were making a statement about race. The misspelled *Yvonne* in me thinks they really uncovered the side effects of ghetto. Still, when your mom is an Oscar-winning actress, it is not really a first name like Apple that matters, but your last name.

Along the street I hear everyone spilling their most private details to the public via cell phones. I've heard a married guy give the play-by-play of his night with his girl on-the-side. I've heard lawyers give the play-by-play of client-privilege conversations. I've heard people lie to their bosses about their whereabouts. I've heard children sass out their mothers. One Friday night at Target a man on his cell phone could even be heard getting (too) excited replaying the details of what "had happened" after someone yelled "Fiiiiiiiiight." (That is ghetto talk for "congregate." As in "Folks! Run! This way *now!*"—which they do the moment the *F* of *Fiiiiiiiight* is uttered. Actually this was Brooklyn, so instead of "Fiiiiiiiight," that night in the Target someone actually yelled "Guuuuuuuuun." And everyone started running *toward* the action.) Afterward, one of those who ran toward the action was boasting on his cell phone about the moment. "It's poppin'! It's poppin'!" he said with a smile. "I had never been that close! *(Smile.)* It was great! *(Smile.)* I felt bad. *(Smile.)* — there was so much blood. But *(smile)* . . ." (Ghetto.)

Forty-five minutes after I set foot on the subway, I finally reach the elevator to my office. On my way up I am greeted by a guy from the sales side with a please-baby-please stare. I clutch the *People* magazine tight, think of the corner where my ghetto journeys began, and realize that I haven't gotten too far away at all.

I am ghetto.

I am not ghetto.

I am you.

That's so ghetto . . .

What We Say

"I seen" as in "I seen that movie," "I seen him before," and the all-purpose "I seen it." Ditto for *did*. "I just got my hair did."

Adding an *-ed* or *-t* to the end of a word that's already in the past tense (tooked).

Saying it (too) loud and (too) proud. This includes spilling details of private lives, private moments, and all foulmouthed commentary in public.

Yelling at your boo in the middle of the street.

Using the walkie-talkie feature on your cell to discuss personal drama in order to save minutes.

Talking on your cell phone while being examined by the doctor.

Talking on your cell phone while at work, especially at jobs where you are supposed to be dealing with customers or the public, as in parking attendants, cashiers, postal workers.

Talking on your cell phone to say a whole lot of nothing.

Ever uttering . . . "Nigga," "My Nigga," "Nigger," "N-word," "Bitch," "Ho," "Motherfucka," "Babydaddy/mama," "Keeping it real."

Using your baby's name as an opportunity to give a shout-out to your favorite luxury brand. Children bearing the names Armani, Dior, Courvoisier, Hennessy, and Lexus (there were actually 1,263 babies named Lexus born in the year 2000) are roaming preschools across the country, according to the Social Security Administration.

1

LIVIN' LARGE

The thought police were at it again.

Around my way the thought police is the block party. Not the organized neighborhood celebration that makes appearances in Hollywood films attempting to depict an idealized New York. But par-tay over here, par-tay over there. The kind of unruliness that comes from alcohol and a boomin' system that can make any block a party.

A par-tay is never that hard to find because every ghetto vehicle has a system. If only one thing works in the ride it will be the radio, souped up and customized so that it no longer resembles a car radio but should be in a club, and thus has to appropriately be called "a system." I was tailgating a Mr. Softee truck one Friday night to remind my thirtysomething bones what it was like to go out again and shower myself in the music from *its* system. Welcome to my ghetto.

As the ice cream truck snaked its way through Brooklyn, Lil' Jon's trademark "Okaaaaaay" screamed from its speakers. You could almost see the entire block bounce. If that wasn't enough to put the sighting in the ghetto hall of fame, the truck had been turned into a booty billboard on wheels. Literally. Instead of pictures of Good Humor choices, the enterprising driver had sold his truck sides and turned the vehicle into one of those mobile advertisements. This Mr. Softee was a moving billboard for Apple Bottoms—Nelly's clothing line to celebrate the, uh, curves of a woman's body.

Nelly held a Miss Apple Bottoms contest on VH1 when he launched the clothing line a few years ago. The show attracted young women from across the country eager to appear on TV butt-first so that Nelly and his entourage could rate their booties. Most of the women didn't even get their faces on TV as the camera stayed at hip level. It gets worse. Here's how VH1 actually described the show in its official press release:

> Multiplatinum artist Nelly is not alone in his love of a
> woman's curves. But few urban entrepreneurs have taken
> their affections to the next level quite the way St. Louis repre-
> senter Cornell Haynes has. Following tightly on the heels of
> the runaway success of his men's line, Vokal, Nelly wanted
> to capitalize on the momentum and still kick it up another
> notch yet with his women's line, Applebottoms. So the idea
> of a Vegas blowout launch after a six-city tour culling six fi-
> nalists with serious junk in their respective trunks from across
> the land of Oh Bootyful, for Spacious Thighs was born.
>
> *(Inside)Out: Nelly: The Search for Miss Applebottoms* fol-
> lows the minds and bulging eyes behind the coast-to-coast
> scouring for a regular girl with an irregular waist-to-ass ratio.
> Thousands of women came out to show him what they was
> working with but only one would win. VH1 followed Nelly
> and his Team Lunatics cohorts as they scoped every jiggle,
> bounce and strut that swings their way to find the new
> "booty" behind their new clothing line. From the Big Apple
> to the City of Angels and everywhere in between, from the
> show to the after-party to the hotel lobby, from bushels of

apples to applesauce, it's all there. VH1 gives you an all-access pass for ass. Enjoy.

Enough said.

Except if that is how they are addressing journalists, can you imagine the level of pathology and disrespect that is slung when the network interacts with the young knuckleheads they are actually trying to get to watch these shows? Nothing exists in a vacuum, either. VH1 is owned by Viacom, one of the largest media companies in the nation. The corporate giant is large enough to own MTV, BET (they made Bob Johnson a billionaire), Nickelodeon, Comedy Central, and Paramount Pictures. When you digest all that *they* are working with, then there really cannot ever be enough said about that all-access pass for ass, can there?

So the Mr. Softee, with the system, was covered in larger-than-life pictures of arched backs and booty as it greeted kids lined up for their soft serve. (It was still an ice cream truck after all.) Par-tay.

The system is so important because music is the most effective weapon of the thought police. There is a point at which if you play music *loud* enough, you will not be able to do anything—including thinking—but bop your head along. The guys with the system know that threshold instinctually. It is as if allowing the block to get stirred up by its own thoughts is a danger that can't be allowed.

One of the methods of torture at Abu Ghraib prison in Baghdad got little attention amid the revelations of the pyramids of naked prisoners, hooded detainees, simulated sex acts, and The Leash; it was "exposure to loud music." Really. Comb through military reports and you'll find that it wasn't the first time this tactic had been used. Loud music was also a favorite form of torture used at Guantánamo Bay prison in Cuba. At Abu Ghraib, Iraqi prisoner Khraisan al-Abally testified that while he was bound and blindfolded, he was also kicked, forced to stare at a strobe light, and blasted with "very loud rubbish music." "I thought I was going to lose my mind," said al-Abally, a burly thirty-nine-year-old man whose wrists were still scarred from plastic cuffs more than a month after his release.[1]

So I was at home trying not to lose my mind when the par-tay outside began. Even my bones were vibrating to Fat Joe's "Lean Back" (the album version with every explicit lyric intact, of course). My husband bobbed past me on his way to the kitchen. Our minds tried to resist even as our heads still bounced, in unison. As I struggled to write, to read the paper, to make my "to-do lists" even, I started thinking about the meaning of ghetto.

The easiest thing to believe is that ghetto is a class. That makes it easy for us to distance ourselves, talk about those people and them. Because no matter how low on the economic totem pole we actually are, ghetto is those folks underneath us.

But ghetto is not a class but a mind-set. And that is the problem. Not every have-not is ghetto and not all the haves are ghetto-free. Ghetto is a mind-set that we all have to fight to get out of.

Because ghetto is a state of mind, it is hard to define but easy to recognize. A good friend of mine is in a mixed marriage. Their differences have nothing to do with her southern African American roots and his Caribbean ancestry. Nor do they stem from the fact that he was raised in Europe and she in the States. Instead she complains to me all the time that she is in a mixed marriage because in her mind her husband is ghetto and she's, well, not. Without explanation I just accept that she is probably right.

At its heart, though, ghetto is thinking short-term instead of long-term. Today is the most important because tomorrow doesn't matter.

During my travels I didn't want to discover that this was true. I failed. "Sometime it feels like I got to get mine right now or it ain't gonna be get," said Eric,* sitting on the stoop outside his Brooklyn home a few blocks from mine. It is the middle of the day and the sixteen-year-old should be in school. His face looks tired and much older than it is. I broke eye contact to try to hide my surprise when he told me his age. He is constantly rhyming under his breath, grooving to a beat that only he hears. There is no telling how long Eric will continue to sit on his stoop: I suspect it ain't gonna be get, then.

Not everyone I talked to on the corners expressed such hopelessness. But enough did. The shrinks and self-esteem repairmen will tell you that sometimes if you hear something enough it doesn't really matter anymore if it isn't true. It becomes truth. And Madison Avenue has certainly put its cash behind the tomorrow-doesn't-matter message.

In 2005 Reebok came up with a flashy ad campaign dubbed "I am what I am." With apparently no memory of Popeye, the hard-to-miss billboards instead displayed stunning portraits of celebrities and athletes spouting irreverent one-line comments that tried to express more who these people are than what they are selling. My favorite of the series showcased Mark Zupan, a tattooed quadriplegic athlete who was the center of the documentary *Murderball* about the rough sport of wheelchair rugby. Zupan is shown in a custom-made wheelchair that looked dark and dangerous and bad-ass, his billboard quote reading: "I play wheelchair rugby. What's the worst that can happen—I break my neck? Again?" Sure, the I-can-do-anything spirit was uplifting. But I liked the dark humor. I saw the billboard only once—when I went to the Reebok Web site. The "I am what I am" billboard that I saw most often around my way featured 50 Cent with his stale, trying to be badass frown. His quote, displayed against a police fingerprint sheet, read: "Where I'm from there is no Plan B. So take advantage of today because tomorrow is not promised." Of course, how could we forget?

---

* Almost all names have been changed in my ghetto journeys to protect the guilty and, more important, so I don't get sued.

The truth about thinking short-term is that it has consequences. The first time I met Sanjay, a teenager from Bed-Stuy, I thought his name was Mohamed. That is what the high school sophomore, whose parents had emigrated from India, is called around my ghetto. Immediately, Sanjay didn't seem to fit in, and it wasn't that he was a minority in a predominantly Black neighborhood. At first I thought that maybe he was just the class nerd—bearing demarcations that my grown-up eyes couldn't see anymore. True, Sanjay is completely out-of-date from head to toe in his choice of clothes. His no-name jeans cling too tight on his skinny frame, the polar opposite of the baggy denim we are used to seeing hanging off teenage butts. In fact, his jeans reminded me of the dark straight-cut boys Lee's that my mom used to get from the discount store and hem up herself for me to wear when the rest of the girls in my class were sporting formfitting designer duds like Jordache and Sassoon. Tucked into Sanjay's jeans is usually a short-sleeve plaid shirt with a collar—something I somehow don't think Jay-Z had in mind when he called for button-ups. His sneakers also stood out not so much because they were name-brand rip-offs but because the white leather was worn and dingy as if he had plucked the shoes from the lamppost graveyard.

Back in the day in neighborhoods like mine, sneakers, worn to their last thread, weren't retired to the trash. Instead we tied the shoelaces together and flung the sneakers up to the sky to catch on the lamppost on the corners, or even better the telephone wires that hung over the street. I'm not really sure if we were marking our territory or trying to give our sneakers respect with such a showy burial or both. Officially my parents wouldn't allow us to participate in the ghetto ritual, but that didn't stop my brother and me from wasting one afternoon desperately trying to throw our matching Nike rip-offs high enough to reach the post. It is harder than it looks and not much fun.

Seeing Sanjay's worn soles, my memory hit rewind and it all came flooding back. Donna Summer even started spinning in my head.

(Didn't you know? Sound tracks to memories are always old-school.) During my ghetto journeys I discovered that the tradition has been updated. I was walking in Lower Manhattan exploring the streets in the heart of NYU territory. There, amid the elegant town houses bordering Washington Square Park, I spotted two cans of Red Bull—tied together and hanging from a lamppost. (Ghetto.) It was a classic case of the remake being worse than the original.

Despite his tight jeans, plaid shirts, and aging footwear, Sanjay's language and swagger is 100 percent hip-hop. Out of sight—heard talking on the phone, for instance—he fits in completely with his peers and surroundings. Still, something just didn't feel right. Then he stumbled into my kitchen one day while I was watching TV. His eyes got as big as the satellite dish on the roof of my house. I was watching *Law & Order* on whatever cable station it happened to be on at the moment. After the signature *L&O* "ba-dump" he asked meekly: "Is this cable?" It was as if he had just sighted a UFO. And it clicked. I knew why Sanjay stood out so much in the neighborhood. He, and his family, were actually living within their means. So his was a life without cable, no new sneakers, no cell phone, no bling bling, no sound system even. In Ghettonation, living within your means just isn't done. There is no need to when you think tomorrow doesn't matter. Not living within your means has become such a blatant problem that even hip-hop has noticed. Missy rhymes in her aptly titled track "Wake Up": "I got the Martin Luther King fever / Ima feed yah what yah teacher need to preach yah / It's time to get serious." "Wake Up" goes on to be the equivalent of a lyrical slap upside the head with its chorus: "If you don't gotta gun (it's alright) / If yah makin' legal money, (it's alright . . .) . . ." Too bad "Wake Up" was never released as a single, because folks surely need the slap. (It's not alright.)

Make no mistake, this issue is not just an urban phenomenon. (Thinking that such behavior exists only in neighborhoods like my Bed-Stuy is, well, ghetto.) My first journalism gig was at a newspaper on the Jersey Shore. The Shore has had its ups and downs. So when I arrived there were definitely some seedy areas to its boardwalk landscape—but nothing that couldn't be made to shine again with a little gentrified TLC. Deal, New Jersey, was one of these little Shore towns wedged between some of the aging neglect that had already been brought back to shining. Every block was filled with huge mint-condition homes with immaculate front lawns. When I would go to take the police blotter for Deal, the cops were almost embarrassed that they wore uniforms when all they could hand over was at most a stolen bicycle incident. At Deal, in contrast to some of its more poverty-stricken neighbors back then, like the cities of Asbury Park and Long Branch, weeks would go by during which there was nothing at all for the police blotter to report. It was the most uneventful 1.2 square miles I had ever experienced. As a proud city girl, honestly I was a little freaked out by its peacefulness. It seemed unnatural to see nothing out of place . . . ever. There was never a toy left on a lawn or even a garbage can untidy. Nothing ever seemed to be off, not even something little. (In the official 2000 Census count 1,070 people lived in Deal—535 men, and 535 women. Really!) Instead it was just huge home, next to huge home, next to huge home.

Then I heard the rumors. The cops actually told me them first. Surrounding towns were eager to spread the gossip, too. The deal with Deal was that those big houses were supposedly empty inside. The rumor was that people would spend so much of their savings buying their big houses that they couldn't afford to fill them with furniture. Deal had a reputation for being all for show. (Ghetto.) Of course, without going into every house there was no way to separate fact from fiction. But the median price of a home in Deal was a little over $1 million while the median household income was only about $58,000. Do the math. It is a good indication that some folks were eating on the floor.[2] The rumor alone, though, was enough to make the point that ghetto had no boundaries. And the city girl in me was eager to believe the rumor since it was the only thing that seemed to make sense of the Stepford-perfect picture.

What makes the ghetto mentality of living for today so disturbing is not just that tomorrow doesn't matter, but that maybe tomorrow could be worse.

Ghetto is also an absence of self-respect. We are at the point where it seems there is no understanding anymore that certain behavior is unacceptable for people who truly love themselves. Ghetto is embracing the worst instead of the best. Call it aiming low.

It was during my commute home from work one day. In the corner of the crowded subway car a child was yelling, "This is a stickup! Hand over your wallets!" He was small, slim, engulfed in a red T-shirt, and his voice still squeaked. He couldn't have been more than nine years old. Maybe it was his giggling, but us grown folks looked up from our papers and in a New York moment no one reacted. There was something so unreal about it all that no one could possibly take it seriously. The child yelled again. This time he waved a gun. It was small, barely peeking out of his small hand. TV taught me it could have been a .22. The giggling didn't stop, though. It could not be real.

"I'm going to shoot.

ONE.

I'm not kidding, I'm going to shoot.

TWO.

What—you don't believe me?

THREE."

Someone screamed. It was another child standing next to the first. The two started to giggle. It was a joke. People buried their heads in their newspapers. The child in the red T-shirt tried to start again with threats to shoot. Even less people paid attention this time. The train conductor came into the car and gave the two an old-fashioned tongue-lashing. He yelled at them like a parent would. All of us in the car cheered.

When the train finally reached the next stop the platform was filled with a dozen or so cops. All had their guns drawn as they peered into the windows as the train slowed. This was no TV episode. Now I was scared. The army of blue stormed our car yelling, "Where's the kid with the red T-shirt? Where's the kid with the red T-shirt?" Newspapers safely in our laps, everyone started pointing. "I didn't do anything," Red-T and his friend, the Screamer, whose part it was to scream, shouted back. "I didn't do anything!"

The cuffs came out and the boys started to cry.

It was the worst joke. The children, with their chests heaving up and down in short bursts and tears streaming down their cheeks, now looked even younger than nine. At one point the cops started yelling at the dim-witted pair for not knowing police protocol. The screamer tried to stick his hands in his pockets to prove he didn't have anything. One cop snatched the child's arm as a frustrated parent would before passing on an obvious life lesson: "Don't stick your hands in your pockets when a cop has his weapon drawn." His tone was as if he just told the kid not to touch the hot stove. The one in the red T-shirt did what was natural and tried to squirm away when the cops started to put the handcuffs on. "Now you're going to resist arrest?" an officer yelled. Another life lesson.

The children left the train with their little hands cuffed behind their backs. I'm still not sure if the gun was real or not. My guess from how the cops handled it when they found it after they patted the kids down is that it was real but wasn't loaded. It doesn't really matter though, does it? We were all just left with "Why?" The car full of grown folks, who could not muster a word when the kid in the red T-shirt first started yelling, now couldn't stop talking. Some argued that the police shouldn't have arrested the screamer accomplice. "He didn't do anything." Others argued that they didn't need to actually cuff the boys at all. People got heated. I couldn't stop thinking of their parents—Mama Screamer and Mama Red-T—picking their sons up at the police station, and I wondered what excuses they would make for them.

The thing is, there is no excuse for such behavior. Instead of making excuses, we should be wondering, why? Why would these children think a fake stickup would be fun? Why is that the behavior they wanted to imitate?

Not only are we embracing the worst but we are also taking pride in doing so. It hit me one morning when I saw a teenager on his way to school in Brooklyn. His backpack was flat empty. He was immaculately dressed in pale-blue and white athletic gear. The crispness of the white was almost blinding. It was as if he had glided above the city's filthy streets to maintain the fabric's virginity. Not a thread was out of place. The loose top laid gently against the baggy sweatpants, which sat precisely just past the shoelaces of the blue-and-white sneakers. The blue-and-white handkerchief around his head deliberately peeked through the rim of the spankin' new cap. Blue and white, blue and white, blue and white. What made the ensemble stand out though was the letterman's jacket, the kind with white leather sleeves, like something out of *Happy Days*. I didn't recognize the school colors immediately. It didn't look like any of the local high schools. And, although close, the colors were a little too powdery for the UNC Tar Heels. What then? When the teen swung his flat pack off for a moment I cranked my head to check out the school name emblazoned across his back. In raised varsity-style print my eyes read GHETTO.

An argument could be made that this pride, this embracing of everything we are, the good as well as the bad, is somehow an aggressive way to erase feeling marginalized, which in the end can be an empowering act. But I'm not going to make that argument. My high expectations won't let me. So instead I shook my head. Not in that oh-yeah-that-makes-sense nod. But in that oh-yeah-that-makes-sense side-to-side swing because sometimes it is just too much.

This brings us back to Lil' Jon. Oh Lord, it is just too much! His songs, like "I Don't Give a [Fuck]" and "Get Low," may be infectious. And granted, pair him up with Usher and Ludacris, suspend any standards for actual songwriting, and you can't get any better than "Yeah!" to bounce your unthinking head to. I do it. Still, there is no question that as the self-proclaimed poster child of Crunk—as in the energy you feel when you are crazy drunk—Lil' Jon is ghetto. It is just a matter of how much. Yet Lil' Jon, who has made exclamation-pointed outbursts a career, is the product of a very stable, middle-class existence. He is a perfect example of aiming low.

Little Jonathan Smith grew up in a four-level house with a pool in a nice neighborhood in southwestern Atlanta. His father was an engineer and his mother belonged to the Army Reserves. He was even a decent enough student, with skill for computers, to be accepted to the area's magnet high school. "We weren't some broke-ass motherf——ers," his manager and childhood friend, Rob McDowell, boasted to *Entertainment Weekly*. "We had go-karts and lots of toys."[3] Proof that ghetto has nothing to do with class but is a mind-set, Jonathan Smith turned into Lil' Jon. And "after graduation," Lil' Jon says, "I was just living in my mom's basement, getting drunk and playing video games during the day, and then going out to DJ parties at night." (Ghetto.)

This does not mean that in the past there weren't those who spent much of their life drunk or high. Drugs ravaged the jazz world, claiming some of its most brilliant performers, including Charlie Parker and Billie Holiday. The difference was that people did not take pride in such behavior. It wasn't something to boast about or celebrate. *Before* his life became a film, how many people realized that Ray Charles was addicted to heroin for most of his career? How many people do *not* know that Snoop Dogg likes to toke up with a fat blunt?

So, no, ghetto is not about class, it is so much worse. It is like a cancer that spreads, uncontrollably transcending class, race, and culture. And life is forever scarred.

Admittedly, part of this "of the moment" culture is the nature of youth. Young foolishness spans every generation. It is necessary to make the rest of us truly feel old. But today we don't seem to be growing up and out of that mind-set. Young adulthood is no longer a phase of development but instead where development ends. And I have started to feel too old way before my time.

The signs that we are refusing to grow up are everywhere. Between 1970 and the most recent census of 2000 the percentage of twenty-four- to thirty-four-year-olds living with parents or grandparents increased by 50 percent to 4 million.[4] The Census Bureau thinks the numbers are on the rise again. And this was *before* the advent of the real estate bubble and rising housing prices. It has come to the point that I just assume without asking that most men in their twenties to about thirtyish still live with their mamas. In fact, New York City, with its skyrocketing real estate prices, leads the nation in this phenomenon. Thirty percent of New Yorkers age twenty-one to thirty-one still live with their parents.

The trend has become so widespread that social scientists are now calling the state between eighteen and thirty-four when many are living at home with little responsibilities "transitional adulthood."[5] And in 2004, *Webster's Dictionary* named *adultescent* its word of the year. **Adultescent** *n.:* an adult who fails to display the maturity and independence expected of a member of his age group.[6] (In other words, those knuckleheads still living at home playing Xbox in the basement.)

Adultescents can have full-time jobs and live with their mothers. Terrell works security in an office building downtown five days a week, plus overtime, with two weeks of vacation, but happily lives in his mother's home in Brooklyn with his teenage younger brother.

They can be fathers themselves and still live with their moms. Anthony, the guy who delivers my packages at work, used to try to convince me that the fact that he was thirty-four years old and still living at home was no big deal, suggesting it was me who was the weird one for moving out as soon as I was legal. "Of course, I live with my mom," he would say, as if no other alternative had ever occurred to him. Besides, he explained, it was convenient to live with Mom because she "likes" to watch his son when his babymama drops the child off a few times a month. Of course, he lives with Mom.

And they can even have college degrees and live with their mommy. I came across James a few years ago. He was thirty years old, an appellate court lawyer in Brooklyn, working fifty-hour weeks doing research to help judges decide cases while living with his parents in Queens, sleeping in the same bedroom he had in high school. His varsity baseball trophies still covered every bit of shelf space. His mother packed lunch for him a few times a week. On weekends he went drinking and clubbing with his two best friends, both also with good jobs. All were still living at home without shame.

James, Anthony, and Terrell are just as ghetto as Lil' Jon, living in his mom's basement after graduating high school, "getting drunk and playing video games" all day.

Living life as a child is the physical manifestation of the of-the-moment mentality. The problem when folks refuse to grow up is that society doesn't grow up, either. Socially, I'd say, we as a society are stuck somewhere right after puberty; the purgatory stage of all hormones and impulse; self-reflection and reasoning have not yet developed. Who knows what the long-term effects of such a continuously spinning pause in development might be. But anyone who has put a needle on a record knows that when it inevitably gets stuck you have to bump it along, otherwise the repetition—of even the most satisfying beat—can drive you mad.

...

I never thought I would feel old enough to say "when I was a kid . . ." but when I was a kid it seemed our biggest fear was our parents. Specifically, getting in trouble. No one wanted to get into trouble with their parents. As kids we had a healthy sense of fear that kept us from doing some things because of the parental repercussions. My dad was overly strict, so my fear was high, but even in those houses that didn't seem to have any rules there was a point where there was something you didn't do because of your parents.

Growing up, Danielle lived around the corner from me. Her mom was a single parent always trying to make ends meet. The phone got turned off so many times that by the time we were in junior high they did not have a phone at all. It meant Danielle spent her days after school at the pay phone on the corner. Every so often her mom would come to our apartment to make a long-distance call to her family back in France. Danielle's mom came to the States as a flight attendant and never took the return flight home. She spoke with a rich French accent that her American kids did not inherit and which was way too exotic for my working-class neighborhood.

Compared to Danielle, I looked like a child because I was. She was wearing lipstick in the fifth grade, smoking in the seventh grade, dyeing her hair in the eighth grade, and completely done with a child like me by the ninth grade. In the sixth grade she was dating high school boys. In high school she was dating grown-ups. After she opted for a GED instead of a cap and gown, all that was left to date were the dirty old men.

I never thought of Danielle by herself. Attached in my mind were her little brother and mom, who talked to my parents. Because of this connection, I guess, I never bought the grown-up act. And I think Danielle appreciated that she could put out her cigarette and still be the sixth-grader with me.

But even Danielle had limits. She wouldn't puff away at the dinner table or tongue down her boy toys in front of her mom. She put on most of her makeup on the bus ride to school, and her swagger was different from 8 a.m. to 3 p.m. than it was when my parents would see her with her mom on the weekends. Even the bravest girl in my world worried about "getting in trouble."

I often find myself wondering if the children of Ghettonation still worry about that—getting in trouble—or is that some quaint old-school concern that is no longer relevant? "When I was growing up, making the right choice was more straightforward," said Jamie Mahaffey, a high school basketball coach in Cincinnati. Mahaffey's face has been plastered all over ESPN because the NBA-bound number one– and number two–ranked high school ball players in the country were on his team. Mahaffey is more concerned with building great men than great players. His mantra for the team is that in life these young men must always "do for themselves." They have Mahaffey's cell on speed dial for their required check-ins throughout the day to ensure they keep out of trouble. And players complain that the mandatory group study sessions he supervises can be tougher than practice. The coach's sessions have helped create a high school basketball team with not only the number one– and number two–top-ranked players in the country, but also a team that has a grade point average of 3.3 among all its players. The toughest part of spending his career around teenage boys, Mahaffey said, is "the choices." That is, helping his boys "make the right choices." "I never wanted to embarrass my parents. I would never do anything that would. That is how my choices were made." I nodded my head because I knew what he meant. I too was taught growing up that I was a reflection of my parents. If I did bad, my parents looked bad. So I did good. Coach Mahaffey thought that is the biggest thing that has changed. "They don't care if they embarrass their parents," he spat out in total disbelief. I nodded my head again because I knew what he meant.

Why would getting in trouble be a concern when we are living in a world where such behavior is what's celebrated? Rap sheets and bullet wounds increase record sales. Celebrities make bigger headlines with their misbehavior than with their craft. Pop stars' criminal trials attract groupies. Athletes write books about their steroid use. And business execs are granted TV shows when they get out of jail. If that is the behavior that we, as a society, are constantly rewarding, then it is no wonder that Red-T and the Screamer would rather imitate what they see on the corner than the behavior of a subway car full of hardworking people coming home from work.

The worst part, though, is that Red-T and the Screamer aren't the only ones drawn to the corner. Having heard that I was trying to write about ghetto, RK Byers, a writer and hip-hop journalist, sent me an e-mail one day. At the time, I didn't know who RK was, but his message in my inbox didn't surprise me because by then I had been getting lots of e-mails from folks wanting to share their "ghetto stories." His story, though, I couldn't get out of my mind.

The subject of his e-mail read "I'm Not From the Hood!?!?!?!?!?!?!?" RK grew up in Nyack, New York, a small, quaint suburban town along the Hudson River a little north of New York City. With its antique shops and quaint downtown, it is the spitting image of cute. It is the town that the closeted Rosie O'Donnell used to talk about endlessly on her show as the perfect place to raise her kids. For RK, Nyack was nothing to boast about. Instead, in his ongoing misguided battle to prove his Blackness, RK tried to obliterate his cute hometown from his DNA. "Throughout these years, of course, my greatest joy would have been to have been taken or mistaken as somebody, you know, *street*," he wrote. My ghetto antenna perked up and I read on. "But over time and with my chameleon ability to ape speech patterns and mannerisms, I began to put on what would have been in the hands of a white person a minstrel show. I became an exaggeration of every ghetto stereotype I'd ever witnessed or heard. I started taking copious amounts of drugs, I got myself a baby-mama, I even traded in my white-collar job for work as a bike messenger."

Reading RK's admission was like striking gold for my ghetto explorer side. His words were downright paralyzing.

I almost couldn't finish reading RK's e-mail. He was no different from Red-T and the Screamer. But the journey was not over, so I read on. Then, unexpectedly, I hit gold, again. It seems RK had a wake-up call. Well, I'll let him tell it. . . .

It was on our way back from a game of one-on-one basketball (which I won), where my opponent, a guy from Harlem named Will, launched into one of his sonnets on life.

"Now Byers, I'm from the hood," he began as we pedaled down Ninth Avenue. "And I *know* you're from the hood."

"I'm not from the hood!" I screamed. I then went on to explain to him where I was from. And in the process, reminded myself.

RK's confusion of ghetto for Black made me wonder about identity. My brain wanted to know what identity means for each of us. My heart wanted to know what's ghetto got to do with it. John L. Jackson Jr., the anthropologist at Penn who reminded me that we all know ghetto, has spent more than a decade trying to wrap his big brain around the issue of identity. In his book *Real Black: Adventures in Racial Sincerity,* Jackson argues that the meaning of race has more to do with what is on the inside, our shared hearts, our shared beliefs, our shared experiences, than just the color of our skin. Jackson's primary focus is race—what does it mean to be Black? But his ideas about identity—its fluidity and changing definition—can be translated to ghetto as well. Too often ghetto is used as a substitution for Black. In his own words RK admitted to becoming "an exaggeration of every ghetto stereotype I'd ever witnessed or heard," thinking this would make him more Black. He was wrong; Black and ghetto are not synonymous. RK's self-propelled race to the bottom and his celebration of the worst didn't make him more Black.. It made him ghetto. A mind-set has fluidity. That is why Apple's mama Gwyneth can be just as ghetto as the knuckleheads I pass every morning on the corner, and suburban Deal, New Jersey, can be just as ghetto as Bed-Stuy. Leave it to a professor to teach us a lil' somethin', somethin'.

The thought police were still outside my door. In my own attempt to beat them I've become obsessed with my thinking. Which means I can't clear my head about any of this—about Sanjay, about Red-T, about Mr. Softee, about the GHETTO letterman jacket. But as much as I think about it all, it still doesn't make sense, and I'm not sure if I can blame that on the thought police. The most depressing thing about all of this is that ghetto, for many of us, is a choice. That is why RK's words are so hard to forget.

Unable to hold on any longer, I'm about to surrender to the thought police and par-tay when it hits me. Maybe that's not so depressing. Choices can be changed, even bad ones.

Awake yet?

How We Look

Wearing acrylic nails so long that a pencil is needed to do the work of the finger. As in pressing the keys on the cash register or scratching a weave.

Wearing a do-rag . . . on dress-down day, to school, to court.

Opting for gold teeth, period.

Dressing for work like you are going to a club.

Dressing for a club like you are working the corner.

Wearing suggestive messages like JUICY or SEXY spread across the butt or chest (because clothes are too tight) if you are under eighteen . . . or if you're over eighteen.

Wearing house slippers outside the house.

And Inside . . . What We Eat
This list can be endless, but these few offenses are just too ghetto not to mention.

Drinking Kool-Aid, and especially, gulping it from a mayonnaise jar.

Eating at Mickey D's for breakfast, lunch, and dinner.

Living on chicken wings from the Chinese take-out joint.

2

EXPORTING DIRTY LAUNDRY

When ODB, as in Ol' Dirty Bastard, died, there
was no Aaliyah-like caravan of doves and carriages.
There were no Biggie tears of loss or musical trib-
utes; there were no Tupac conspiracy theories, no
Jam Master Jay head shaking, or Big Pun shock. At
thirty-five years old the former Wu Tang Clan rapper collapsed in his studio, and life for most of us
went on. Even in the hip-hop community ODB
was always out there—the Flavor Flav with skills.
No matter what name he went by—ODB, Dirty,
Dirt McGirt, or my personal favorite, Big Baby
Jesus—Russell (Rusty to his family) Jones was hard
to miss. That is why the rather subdued end of his
life stood out for me. I wouldn't go so far as to say
that I was a big fan of the rapper, but I have to admit the irony of his death compared to his life did
hit me, so I couldn't stop thinking about BBJ.

Perhaps it was because he was responsible for the best ride of my
life, literally. One summer somewhere between his Wu Tang days and
Mariah Carey cameos I ran into Dirty at Coney Island in Brooklyn.

One of my favorite ghetto loves every summer is trips to Coney Island. The urban beach and amusement park have a long history of seediness. My grandfather used to talk about going to Coney Island when he was a teenager as if he were spilling reckless secrets.

"Coney Island was a dirty place," he'd say, shifting his ever-present cigar from one side of his mouth to the other. "But a good time." He didn't really look at my brother or me when he would say "good time." Those days at the beach were before my grandma was in the picture. But since he so rarely talked about himself growing up, we got the point that it was a special place for him. One summer he and half a dozen friends even rented a bungalow at Coney Island during a rare moment of indulgence. After his father died when he was twelve, my grandfather, the oldest of five kids, went to night school so he could work during the day. By fourteen he had grown a mustache to look older and was supporting his entire family. Now that I think of it, I'd imagine that dirty place, with its freedom from responsibility, was definitely a good time. I enjoyed our Coney Island bond since the grandfather I knew always lived in Virginia and not his hometown of New York. "People still go to Coney Island? That was a good time." With that he would poke out his cheek with his tongue—signaling where he expected a kiss from each of his grandchildren—and the conversation was over.

Although Coney Island was originally intended as a private vacation spot for the rich, in 1920 the subway line to the beach was completed, spilling thousands upon thousands of the city's poor just a few steps from the sand.[1] A few years later the private beach was open to the public and the transformation was complete. Old photos from the time show the dingy beach covered in wall-to-wall bodies as holiday crowds could reach over a million. Unable to afford the bathhouses or boardwalk entertainment, they came with their bathing suits under their clothes and food packed from home tucked away in their bags. The tradition is still the same today.

Because we had no car, Coney Island was the beach of choice for my family when I was growing up. Like the masses six decades before, every weekend the four of us would hop on the subway weighted down by shopping bags of food. My mom would get up early to make sandwiches upon sandwiches (Wonder bread and bologna was my favorite), cold fried chicken wrapped in aluminum foil, deviled eggs, industrial-sized bags of supermarket-brand chips, cookies, and whatever else she could find from our kitchen shelves. My dad would make his special lemonade sweetened to cavity perfection. He was also in charge of carrying the umbrella so we could hide from the sun that we were trekking out to the edge of Brooklyn to get close to. Of course, there was also the System. My dad never actually hoisted it up on his shoulder, but back then the weight of any boom box made just carrying it enough of a workout. Our system had a mini TV with a two-inch screen. (The theme song for these beach memories has got to be "We Are Family," Sister Sledge.) My brother and I were in charge of the blanket. (Ghetto families never sit on a towel at the beach when you can treat the sand like a bed with a queen-sized blanket or sheet.) We would then drag our cargo in a shopping cart (ghetto) across the sand to the perfect spot, which always seemed to take my dad too long to find. Eating and the beach were so intertwined in my mind that I was a bit stunned later in life when I came across non-ghetto beaches that had no-food-on-the-sand rules and even no-music warnings! At my first sight of the red NO signs I think I even gasped in shock.

Despite my fondness for the sandwiches and sand, the best part of our day at Coney Island was when the sun started to go down and my parents would treat my brother and me to the rides. Coney Island's old-school carnival rides up against the dirty boardwalk are still what I measure all amusement parks by. The Cyclone, with its wooden track and rickety noises and torn leather seats, will beat out the biggest loop-the-loop suburban metal coaster any day. As an adult I haven't set foot on Coney's Island's dirty sand in decades but I still visit the boardwalk amusement park once a summer. The nation's original Nathan's is still there, but these days its neighbor is a Popeye's chicken, which makes perfect sense in a ghetto kind of way.

The charm of Coney Island is that the rides push the limit to the point that you fear for your life, or should. Faster, longer, more dangerous. That is the fun. So it is fitting that at this grungy edge of Brooklyn, ODB, one of hip-hop's bigger stars, would be standing in line for a ride like the rest of us. The ride was actually the Music Express—a roller-coaster-like train that went around a circular track set to music. At your suburban amusement parks anyone with a little thrill thirst just plows on past this staple of a ride because it doesn't leave the ground. But in ghetto circles the Music Express is prime entertainment because the speed is always so dangerously fast it doesn't matter that the train doesn't leave the ground. Gravity, because it squishes riders together in the same car, forces couples to snuggle and cheap feelies are unavoidable. (I think the first time a boyfriend and I made it past first base was on the Music Express, thanks to gravity.) And the reason the guy who boards alone—there is always one—and sits with his hands in the air like he just don't care is so he can prove that he doesn't miss the cheap feelies that come from being pressed up against a shorty sharing the seat.

The other reason the Music Express is the ride of choice in ghetto circles is the System. At this ride at Coney Island there is a separate DJ booth worthy of a club and local talent typically spins. Par-tay over here, par-tay over there. Everyone bounces in mindless unison. It is a toss-up who is having more fun—those on the ride, or the crowd dancing nearby. Even if you are not planning to ride, part of ghetto etiquette is to at least be seen bouncing by the scene of the Music Express. Then when the par-tay is just getting hot, the kid at the control booth inevitably flips the switch to make the ride go backward and hats, hair, and weaves start flying.

One day ODB was in the car in front of me on the Express. To show this international star some Brooklyn hometown love, the DJ mixed into overtime and we got the longest ride of our life, clocking in at sixteen minutes. As a roller-coaster junkie I will always be grateful.

Because of that "bond," when the thirty-five-year-old star passed away, I noticed. I admit it. I felt like I knew him, just a little bit. Or at least knew where he was from. His trip to Coney Island made me feel like on some level we were from the same place. And his age, so close to my own, made me feel like we could still be in the same place. I read everything I could get my hands on about his death, like some kind of desperate junkie, trying to make sense of how he ended up in such a different place instead. Then, finally, I scored.

"But as O.D.B.," the *New York Times* reported in its surprisingly on-going multiday coverage of his passing, "he was also comfortable spinning a public mythology, saying, for example, that he had grown up on welfare, or that he had not known his father."

You see, neither was true.

"Our brother looked at things as selling records," said his sister Monique Jones. "So he dismissed whatever lies he told as just a way of getting publicity."[2]

Jackpot. The most devastating part of ghetto is that it sells.

From Dy-no-mite to BET, and everything in between, people may wrongly assume it is a Black thang, but ghetto products are consumed not just in the ghetto but also across the nation and around the globe. On Japanese TV, it has gotten to the point where a running character sure to get a laugh is the one "who acts ghetto," wearing baggy jeans, hat turned back, spouting *awiiiit* and *nigga* (which is not bleeped out or swapped for the N-word).[3] According to the Internet news mill, there is a hip-hop clothing store in Malawi, Africa, called Niggers. Blogger David Sylvester was making a charity bike trip with a group across Africa when he stumbled upon the shop. At the sight of the Black American cyclist, the Malawian shopkeeper "thumbed his chest and said 'P. Diddy, New York City! We are the niggers!' "⁴ If it wasn't for the photo of the store with its clear NIGGERS signage featured in Sylvester's blog, I could have convinced myself the scene didn't exist. (For the few—I hope—of you who don't get it: "I have traveled all over the world," writes Sylvester in his niggers blog. "I have never seen a store by the name of 'Jew Devils,' 'Spic Bastards,' 'Muff Divin' Dykes' or anything like that—*only* the store 'Niggers.' ") And Gizoogle.com, a ghetto Google that translates your Internet searches into Snoopspeak, gets more than 60,000 hits a day.⁵

Within hours of ODB's death, a memorial page went up on the Web filled with talk from folks in New Zealand to Serbia to Argentina of tipping forties for the man with the fake welfare credentials. More than seven thousand people from around the world sent e-mail wishes. Doug from Scotland planned to smoke a blunt every day in the rapper's memory. Dudek from Poland wrote that he would miss ODB because he was the best "NIGGA 4 EVER AND EVER AND EVER," and Nico from France says simply: "Repose en Paix, Nigaz."⁶

Hip-hop does not have to be ghetto, but these days it sure is doing its best to be. (I'd like to go one day without hearing about 50 Cent's gunshot wounds, Lil' Jon's Crunk cup, or The Game's beef.) What makes today's hip-hop ghetto is that, unfortunately, from content to images it has become a genre that celebrates the lowest common denominator. Or at least a genre that *sells* when it celebrates the low points.

A distinction must be made between radio hip-hop and digging-in-the-crates hip-hop. Radio hip-hop is pop music. It consists of the singles anyone can hear over and over again without any effort or education about hip-hop. It is also the videos we see over and over again. It is the magazine covers and the sound tracks to movies. Hardcore hip-hop folks will tell you that what we hear on the radio is not true hip-hop. For those who feel the beat in their bones 24/7, those who are faithful to mix tapes and out-of-the-trunk albums and underground rhymers, the watered-down, commercialized version of radio hip-hop the rest of us rag on about is a different species.

My brother is a jazz musician. It can be a heartbreaking calling for a young man to be devoted to a music that is, well, dying. The audience these musicians play for is aging, which means that it is constantly shrinking. My brother's biggest beef is that most of us don't know the true meaning of jazz. Instead, it has come to be the catchall musical term used for any and all instrumental music. Whenever he comes over to my house he takes a peek at the BET Jazz Channel. It is usually no more than a couple of minutes before it has pushed him into a rage. (Kind of like the regular BET does for me.) That's because in his mind, the mind of a dedicated student and faithful jazz lover, when he turns on the BET Jazz Channel (or anything with the generic label of jazz) he doesn't think he hears any jazz. R&B—sure; a little gospel—yeah, even reggae; instrumental Muzak—too often; and sometimes, if he is lucky he hears blues, but not what he ever considers to be true jazz. "If I thought this was what jazz is, I wouldn't like it, either," he yelled one day at the TV when an advertisement came on for a jazz festival in Jamaica. The top acts were John Legend, Al Green, and Shaggy. If you've heard Coltrane, Bird, or Monk, then you could never dream of putting the Jamaica festival lineup in the jazz category. The difference between John Legend and John Coltrane is the difference between radio hip-hop and digging-in-the-crates hip-hop. Those who truly live the music will tell you that, like jazz, digging-in-the-crates hip-hop is overflowing with thoughtful rhymes, political commentary, rebellious prose, and emotion.

While I fully understand the differences between radio hip-hop and true hip-hop, it doesn't really matter. Most folks will never hear the digging-in-the-crates hip-hop. That is because radio hip-hop is what sells and sells and sells. The reality is, it is the only hip-hop most of us know.

Radio hip-hop is not the first or the only music that has showcased the worst. Popular music has always pushed the limits of comfort. I was a teenager in the eighties, and the MTV of my youth consisted of endless hours of heavy-metal hair bands with names like Ratt, the Scorpions, and Poison. Hairspray and perms were as necessary as guitars, and the videos also favored big-haired, scantily clad women. Tawny Kitaen was an early video ho, making a career of writhing on a car hood. But how different is Kitaen from, say, today's self-proclaimed proudest video ho Karinne Steffans, aka Superhead? (Yes, her nickname means just what your dirty mind thinks it does.) Both started with a mediocre movie credit (*Bachelor Party* vs. *A Man Apart*), both got their fame in videos (Whitesnake vs. Jay-Z, Mystikal, R. Kelly), and both dated like sport through their respected music worlds (at one industry party, Superhead showed up on Usher's arm with nothing more than a bathrobe on). Kitaen clinched her ghetto credentials when she reportedly keyed another woman's SUV in a jealous catfight. While Superhead calls herself Superhead. Enough said. They're not different—both be ghetto.

So hip-hop is not the first. The difference is the power of influence that hip-hop holds now, which far surpasses the mass cultural domination of any preceding commercial music form. Hair bands never came close to replacing the dominant image of white men. Instead they remained a slice of the music industry. But hip-hop *is* our mainstream now. Its language, its images, its content, and its rules have become American culture. Snoop Dogg and aging corporate titan Lee Iacocca spout Fo shizzle dribble together on TV spots to sell Chryslers!

Our favorite ghetto mama, Gwyneth Paltrow, admitted that even baby Apple is a big hip-hop fan despite the fact that her father is part of the rock band Coldplay. "She loves music. It's weird though, 'cause she's very, very into hip-hop. She loves Jay-Z," said Paltrow of her sixteen-month-old daughter. "She loves *The Black Album*. It's just so funny, because she's like this little white cherub with the blond hair and big cheeks and then you put on '99 Problems' and she's rocking her head . . . She loves it."[7] While most of the entertainment press made a big deal out of Apple's liking hip-hop, that part didn't surprise me. A baby likes repetitive beats, which means Jay-Z wins every time, even if Apple's daddy is a rock star. What stood out for me more was that Hollywood's own beloved "white cherub with blond hair," Gwyneth, owns *The Black Album*. And the fact that she plays "99 Problems," as in "99 Problems and a bitch ain't one," for her sixteen-month-old, makes her, well, ghetto.

Hip-hop references slip out of the most unsuspecting places. I was rapid channel-surfing one night, barely sticking to one station for more than thirty seconds, when I heard something from the tube that made my thumb come to a halt. It was "Biaaaaaaatch." On the screen was not the raucous comedy of *Chappelle's Show* or the musical party of *106 and Park* or even the grit of *Law & Order*, but the scene was a harmless sitcom with two white suburban elementary-school-age boys sitting on the floor playing video games. I was channel-surfing so by definition don't remember the specific show, but it was definitely part of ABC's "wholesome" TGIF lineup. (Unfortunately, my ghetto self thinks all *those* shows, well, look alike.) It was the boys' excitement over the game that called for the "Biaaaaaaatch," in its full hip-hop intonation. It was not a punch line, it was not a plot twist, or a climatic crossroads; instead it was nothing more than dialogue filler—just how two young boys talk today. "Biaaaaaaatch." Without a pause, the two on screen continued to play their video games and I kept turning the channels.

Some people have traced the commercialization of hip-hop to a moment in 1986. I tend to think development—upward, or in this case, downward—is gradual. If it weren't, then it would be easy to spin back to "how things used to be." But we all know that without a souped-up DeLorean and a crazy mad scientist,* going back in time would be pretty much impossible. Instead, if such a transformation is really go-

---

* Admit it, you remember Michael J. Fox's *Back to the Future*, too.

ing to take hold, flourish, and spread it has many roots like a tree or a weed. Therefore, ultimately pinpointing such a transformation to a single moment can get kind of iffy. Still, 1986 seems to indeed be one of those roots when hip-hop crossed over and became big business.

The moment was during a concert at Madison Square Garden. Headliner Run-D.M.C. took the stage amid the excitement, the screams, and most of all, the beat. The group was the first rap act with a double-platinum album; the first rappers to appear on *American Bandstand* with Dick Clark; the first rap group to get a *Rolling Stone* cover. They were, effectively, the first rap group to cross over. Taking over Madison Square Garden was a symbol of all of that. "This is my house," Run belted, bringing the crowd to its feet. "This is my fuckin' house!"[8] It was. Then Run called for everything to stop, for a moment, and urged the crowd to hold their Adidas sneakers in the air. And 20,000 fans did. Standing backstage were a handful of Adidas executives, invited by Run's brother and the group's manager, Russell Simmons. Afterward the rap trio went on to sign a $1.5 million endorsement deal with the sneaker company.[9] It was a powerful moment. Hip-hop changed forever and there was no going back. Cha-ching.

This is not a rant against hip-hop. That would be too easy. To repeat, hip-hop is not the first or the only music that has showcased the worst. Instead, hip-hop is just the music that the mainstream likes to complain about. Thinking back to the eighties again, when it became widely known that Axl Rose from the famed Guns N' Roses had a fondness for using *nigger* and *bitch* in his songs, it was never used as an indictment of heavy metal as a music, or even an indictment against the band itself since Rose is still hailed as some kind of musical trailblazer. At the time, the actor Sean Penn even wrote an op-ed piece in the *New York Times* coming to the nigger-spouting Rose's defense. Has there ever been such an outpouring of support for, say, 50 Cent, Ludacris, or DMX? Wait, back that thought up, Eminem *did* get a groundswell of support from civil libertarians for the supposed social commentary in his lyrics despite their blatant misogyny and homophobia. But, then, he is also currently the genre's only successful white artist.

Still, even if it is not the first to showcase the worst, hip-hop is the music that thumps through Black neighborhoods and encompasses the Black images that are spit across the world. It is what our children are bouncing their heads to. So as a Black woman living within earshot of what is coming out of the mouths of young Black folks over the radio these days, I can't afford *not* to say something. Especially when the ho-ing of Black women has become big business. Therefore, this is not a rant against hip-hop. Look in the mirror—this is a rant against ourselves.

So in the name of selling records ODB takes on the character of a Black man who grew up on welfare with no daddy because the stereotype is easier for buyers to digest than the reality. In reality Rusty was the product of a loving mom and pop in a close-knit traditional working-class household in Brooklyn.

The ODBs of the world argue that they are just giving the public what they want. And ghetto sells—hip-hop generates $10 billion annually—so the argument has merit.[10] "Hip-hop is a corporation," said Jay "Ice Pick" Jackson, a thoughtful producer and senior VP at Ruff Ryders, speaking on the radio. I had hit the jackpot again, this time listening to NPR (proof again of hip-hop's mainstream credentials). The discussion was hip-hop and its images of women. Ice Pick had the unfortunate role of being the only industry insider and only male guest for the segment. Despite the host's best intentions to force the music exec into a corner, Pick handled himself pretty well, dropping nuggets like these along the way: "Hip-hop is a corporation. It is not a culture anymore. It is all about dollars and cents. When you look at videos you see what sells. Nothing more, nothing less." The host pushed back, demanding to know whether the views of hip-hop videos and lyrics were sexist and misogynist. "I would say," Jackson paused, "they're like the views of America today." The radio announcer seemed almost startled by such truth. "Aren't there any limits?" the exacerbated host shot back. "You have to have limits within self," Ice Pick responded. "People are going to go as far as you let them take it. As long as it is profitable they're going to keep going with it."[11]

And that is the larger point. Why do we buy it? Why do we listen to it? Why do we claim it? Admittedly it is a chicken-or-the-egg puzzle — Did demand create the product or did product create the demand? — that probably can't be resolved. But, given that, perhaps more important than trying to figure out which came first is the why. Why does radio hip-hop sell? Overlooked in that "giving the public what it wants" cop-out is basic supply-side economics. If there is only one product to buy, of course it will sell because customers don't have a choice.

I don't like rice very much. But what if when I went to the market the *only* food available was shelves and shelves of Uncle Ben's? Eventually, I'd learn to like rice, otherwise I'd starve.* When faced with such limited choices, most of us lower our standards and accept something we wouldn't necessarily choose if other options were available.

Of all rap's great talents from Rakim to Nas, the Fresh Prince never comes to mind—for any of us. Then I heard him spit this gem in one of his songs:

> Black radio, they won't play me though
> Guess they think that Will ain't hard enough
> Maybe I should just have a shootout
> just ignorant, attacking, acting rough
> I mean then, will I be black enough?

Granted, not the smoothest flow, but for once I was hung up on something Big Willie had to say. He was talking about choices, or lack

---

* Note: There is a big loophole here for the Condi kind, which I don't think I'd ever be able to stomach.

thereof. I can think of nothing more basic to ghetto than not questioning the choices that we are given.

The other part of the picture that can never be left out when talking about product choice and demand is the marketing muscle behind hip-hop. Because Ice Pick is right, hip-hop is a corporation. If the hip-hop industry generates $10 billion a year, that means there are a lot of corporate suits—since none of these artists (read Black) labels distributes this stuff—who will do what they have to do to ensure that they don't lose that kind of cash. "Some companies don't care what an artist has said to become so popular. It's just can he say it holding the company's phone, wearing its clothes, or driving its car?" says Jackie Rhinehart, former senior vice president of marketing for Universal/Motown Records. "It's all about the money."[12] Sales from hip-hop cell phone ringtones alone earn $400 million and counting. Hits like Snoop's "Drop It Like It's Hot" can have as many as 100,000 to 200,000 downloads a week. Hip-hop DVDs pull in $561 million and product placement $3.46 billion. Hip-hop artists like Snoop, 50 Cent, and Lil' Jon are even now making the full frontal leap into porn, where they are generating $10 billion a year. Snoop's *Doggystyle* video released back in 2001 sold hundreds of thousands of copies in an industry where any video that sells 4,000 copies is considered a big hit. "Everyone has bones in his closet," says Killick Datta, owner of Pony, making no apologies for inking a sneaker deal with a porn king such as Snoop. "But Snoop transcends Hip Hop."[13] The first shipment of Snoop's Doggy Biscuitz shoe line sold out in three days nationwide.

It is because of the undeniable understanding that today's hip-hop is all business that Pharrell of the Neptunes was speaking at Harvard Business School. I was listening from the very back of the packed room when I started to feel sick. It was when the Grammy award–winning producer behind such hits as Nelly's "Hot in Here," Busta's "Pass the Courvoisier," and Mystikal's "Shake Ya Ass" claimed he didn't have any responsibility for the images he creates. When asked about today's videos, he told the Harvard crowd that if "video hos didn't want to shake their ass then they wouldn't have shaked [sic] their ass." Point taken. "I'm an artist not an activist," he protested defiantly. No doubt. "It is not my responsibility." Sickening.

Just when I could have given up hope I was encouraged to hear someone entrenched in the hip-hop world who was also getting sick from it all. "I felt like I was hurting us by doing what I was doing," said AJ Calloway, the former host of BET's 106 and Park, to an audience of Black college students, about his time as host of the video show. AJ's comments made national news, and I had to pinch myself just to make sure I had heard him correctly. By the end of his five-year tenure, AJ was having regrets because of the lewd content that increasingly dominated many of the show's videos. He admitted that he felt that working on the show went against a vow he had made to himself after facing racism growing up to "never do anything against my race." I pinched myself again. "Pick your five favorite songs," he ordered the crowd at South Carolina State University. "Write down every word that's in your favorite songs. Read it back to yourself and think about what that has put into your head."[14] By the time AJ was done my arm felt a little bruised. It was a reminder that, maybe, I am not as old-school as I thought.

It is not just hip-hop music, though. I think one of the most ghetto nights out I have ever had wasn't at a club or on the corner or even on the subway but at a national awards dinner celebrating Black authors. In an aging hotel ballroom attendees crossed picket lines of striking low-paid Black hotel workers for our evening of pomp and circumstance. I was new to the scene and in my naïve idealism, or maybe old-fashioned snobbism, it never occurred to me that the book world could be ghetto. There's no fast cash, no easy money, and most authors lead very isolating, anonymous lives. I was in for a surprise. The evening was an interesting mix with appearances by sci-fi writer Octavia Butler, chick-lit author Tonya Lewis Lee (Spike's wife), and best-selling erotica queen Zane, who was making one of her first live appearances after years of hiding her identity.

"Please sit down, sit, sit, sitiiiiiit." The microphone was squeaking and barely audible. The night had not even started yet, but the woman at the podium already looked exhausted, the way a kindergarten teacher can look during a class trip. With the program almost an hour late getting started the crowd had already gotten rowdy. The line for the cash bar was starting to circle the ballroom. With the event over-booked, there were not enough seats by a long shot, and because of the strike the organizers couldn't do anything fast enough. Literary folk— publishers, editors, booksellers, authors, and, most important, spon-sors—were getting u-gly. It wasn't *The Source* Awards—yet—but neck-swinging exchanges dominoed across the room as people scram-bled for seats. It meant the exasperated pleas from the podium for everyone to "sit sit sit" fell on equally exasperated ears, tired feet, and hungry bellies.

My group secured seats at a makeshift table in the corner by the kitchen door after befriending the hotel chef, who made the mistake of surfacing from the kitchen for a moment to survey the chaos. To make up for the lack of tablecloth and proper place settings, our new friend insisted on giving us a private waiter who would stand in line at the buf-fet for the group and serve us all night. Or it was supposed to be all night. Instead, he served us just one overflowing plate of turkey, all night. My group of strangers and acquaintances ate family-style, with our fingers, since by the time we were seated the ballroom was out of silverware, and, well, hunger, remember, makes you do ghetto things. As I nibbled on my turkey, none of that really fazed me, though. In-stead, my eyes were glued to a few tables directly in front of the podium. It was, for a lack of a better name, the ghetto-ink crowd. Ur-ban fiction, street fiction, hip-hop stories, thug dramas, babymama sagas, some even call it gangsta lit.

Street fiction has been a constant strand in Black literature for decades. The first of such writers was probably Iceberg Slim, aka Robert Beck, who after being released from ten months of solitary confinement at Cook County Jail penned *Pimp: The Story of My Life*, published in 1969.[15] Graphic in both language and subject matter, the book broke narrative ground by capturing Slim's life as a pimp in Chicago in the 1950s. Ice-T pays homage to Iceberg Slim with his stage name. *Pimp* has been translated into French, Spanish, Italian, Dutch, Swedish, and Greek. In the spring of 2001, *Pimp* briefly graced United Press International's top ten mass-market paperback list alongside *To Kill a Mockingbird*, *The Hobbit*, and *Fahrenheit 451*. His next book, *Trick Baby*, was about a mixed-raced hustler dubbed Trick Baby because, obviously, anyone with such heritage had to be the product of Black prostitutes and their white tricks. Slim sold more than 6 million books before his death in 1992, making him one of the biggest-selling Black authors in history.[16]

Donald Goines, also a pioneer in street lit, first read Iceberg Slim while doing his last stint behind bars. The result for Goines, a heroin addict who pimped and robbed to support his habit, was the birth of his first book, *Dopefiend*, an instant ghetto classic published in 1970 that still sells 200,000 copies a year, according to Holloway House, the small publisher in Los Angeles that publishes Goines's books along with those of Iceberg Slim. Goines, who never kicked his drug habit, wrote sixteen books in just under five years. In 1974 while sitting at his typewriter in his home outside Detroit, Goines was shot to death. He died at the same age as ODB, thirty-five years old. In the next room, his common-law wife, Shirley, was also killed. Their two children hid under the couch.[17] The murders were never solved, turning the author into a martyr. Goines is still hailed by rap culture today, frequently referenced in rhymes by a wide variety of artists, from Nas to DMX to Jadakiss to Ludacris.

Although ghetto lit never really died, after its burst in the seventies it was indeed ailing like Blaxploitation films and platform boots until it crossed paths with hip-hop. In 1999 raptivist Sister Souljah resuscitated the genre with her best-selling novel *The Coldest Winter Ever*, a brutal story about a drug dealer's daughter. The success of the book revived ghetto lit, opening the door for a slew of self-published best sellers and start-up Black publishing houses devoted to cranking out books with titles such as *Project Chick, Gangsta Life*, and *Road Dawgz*. A typical tale is a mixture of foul language, bullets, drugs, and in-your-face sex and violence. About the only thing these books tend to be missing is the services of a copy editor to fix the grammar, spelling, and typos.

One of the more successful authors, Vickie Stringer, wrote her first novel while serving seven years in federal prison on drug charges. When she was released in 2001, she sent her manuscript across the publishing world, but mainstream publishers wouldn't touch her book *Let That Be the Reason*. She got twenty-six rejection letters: "They said it was not well written," she says.[18] So Stringer borrowed $2,500, printed 1,500 copies on her own, and began selling them from her car, in beauty salons, and to street vendors. (Sounds like rap back in the day, doesn't it?) Her batch of books sold out in three weeks.

Acknowledging that it had become an underground hit, bookstores began to stock the novel, and within three years her first book had sold more than 100,000 copies. The publishing house she founded, Triple Crown Publications, named for the drug crew she used to run with in Ohio, Triple Crown Posse, is the undisputed leader in the ghetto fiction genre with fifteen authors, including a few still on lockdown whose book jacket photos were taken against the drab gray concrete walls of their jail cells. In the fall of 2004, Stringer, riding around Columbus in her BMW X5, bragged to the *New York Times* that she would pass the millionaire mark by the end of the year.

It took less than five years after Sister Souljah supposedly revived ghetto lit for the genre to overrun Black fiction. Black booksellers sheepishly admit that it often is what is keeping their doors open. (The cringing from book folks comes from the quality of the writing, which most admit is just not very good.) Now mainstream publishers with dollar signs dancing in their heads are trying to take over (as with hip-hop). In 2004 Stringer signed a six-figure two-book deal with Simon & Schuster. And St. Martin's Press has snapped up three Triple Crown authors. One of my finger-eatin' tablemates at the authors' dinner was a manager at a Waldenbooks in Chicago who complained much of the night that the only Black books the chain allows her to order are in the ghetto lit genre. For anything else, from Toni Morrison to Terry McMillan to Paul Beatty to Ellis Cose, she has to fight for shelf space. And usually loses.

That dominance stood out at the Black authors awards dinner. Popping BYOBs of Crystal and Dom P, the ghetto lit crowd was hard to ignore. Personally, I couldn't stop staring at the table upon table upon table of the par-tay over here, par-tay over there.

As a Black writer, part of me was somewhat excited that "writer" and even "publisher" had entered people's dreams alongside rapper and ballplayer. But listening that night to the thirty-fifth title that replaced every S with a Z and hearing about plots that contained some horrific drug-sex-violence triangle, the Black woman in me found it hard to cheer anymore.

Champions of ghetto lit argue that the genre has gotten young Black folks to read and thus should be praised. This is perhaps the most disturbing aspect of the entire phenomenon. When did our standards get so low that we are now satisfied with simply reading? It is like being satisfied that our children are eating vegetables because they pour ketchup on their fries. Nourishment—physical and mental—requires more. Granted, there are worse things folks can be doing than reading trash. But what happens when that is all we are reading?

I was browsing a Black bookstore in Baltimore when a mother and her preteen daughter walked in for their weekly trip. It was payday, which meant the girl, who looked about twelve, got to buy a book. It struck me because, although payday was not a windfall in my house, growing up I did regularly babysit a kid, my brattiest charge, whose mom let him pick out a toy to buy every payday. Here the tradition was a book, which seemed a step in the right direction. The girl in Baltimore headed straight for the Donald Goines collection and was very upset when the book she wanted was out of stock. Instead of straying from the genre, though, she—bratlike, of course—was trying to convince her mom to allow her to get two books next payday instead.

James Fugate, owner of Eso Won Books, a Black bookstore in South Central L.A., has one word for ghetto lit: disturbing. The veteran bookseller is perhaps one of the most outspoken against the trend. "I'm sick of talking about it," he says.[19] "To me people can read what they want to read. I've never been opposed to books by Donald Goines and Iceberg Slim," he admits. "But those books were bridges to other literature." The ghetto lit being written today is mostly "mindless garbage about murder, killing, thuggery." When you read this ghetto lit, he concludes, "nothing happens to your mind."[20] And that is the problem.

Which again brings us back to, why? Fiction is supposed to be the stories our minds create. Why is this the fantasy we are choosing?

My mind was clouding up with so much emotion—why we gotta be like that? It became clear that this was a question that needed to be taken to an expert. Dr. Todd Boyd, a member of the faculty of the School of Cinema and Television at the University of Southern California, is one of those professors who gets props from students for making intellectualism and critical thinking not feel like lectures. He is a regular talking head in the national media, which calls him the "hip-hop professor." (The title of his latest book is *The Notorious Phd's Guide to the Superfly '70s*.) I like to check in with Dr. B now and then because he's like a reality check—an anti-bullshit detector in the flesh. Even on my worst day he is the first to point out that the powers that be are not invincible, and he is a welcome reminder that there are still folks around who are willing to tell it like it is no matter who they piss off.

So I asked the professor, why is ghetto lit the fantasy we are choosing? "The ghetto is drama," he said. "The ills of poverty are far more dramatic than the angst of middle-class life."

It struck me just how universal Boyd's truism was when author James Frey's credibility began to shatter into a million little pieces in the winter of 2006 when his best-selling memoir, *A Million Little Pieces*, about his drug addiction and his rehab struggles, was found to be soaked with untruths. The interesting thing about Frey's embellishments is that he didn't lie to make his life seem better but to make it seem worse. "I am an alcoholic and I am a drug addict and I am a criminal," he wrote repeatedly. One of the most blatant lies that Frey wrote about was the criminal part. He claimed he did a three-month stint in jail for beating up a cop. It never happened. He made up his jail time. Ghetto. At the height of the controversy surrounding Frey's lies he sat down on Oprah's couch. Oprah had already catapulted Frey's book to best-selling status. After getting her stamp of approval *A Million Little Pieces* sold faster than any other book in the history of her famous book club. When news initially broke that maybe Frey wasn't as much of an alcoholic, drug addict, and criminal as he wished he was, the daytime diva even called in to Larry King to defend him. A few weeks later, after the journalism establishment blasted her support, Oprah snatched it back, calling Frey to her show and announcing that she felt "duped" by his deceit.

"I thought of myself as being tougher than I was and badder than I was," the liar told Oprah in his defense. "It helped me cope."

The talk-show queen asked back: "Did you cling to that image because that's how you wanted to see yourself or because that would make a better book?"

"Probably both," Frey responded.

Remember when folks used to lie their way up? Like claiming we made more money than we did, had better jobs than we had, were the hero instead of the sidekick, raised extraordinary beings instead of average ones? Now folks are lying their way downward. And why not? Frey's book was the second biggest seller in 2005 behind only the new Harry Potter. Being a "criminal" sells. Ghetto.

Despite my tendency to see our ghetto ways as something that is just now consuming us, according to Dr. B the 1970s were the point when things actually shifted. Ghetto became the focus. "Poverty came to define Black authenticity," he said. "Poor Black people were thought to be more 'real' than their newly liberated middle-class relatives." At the time Curtis Mayfield, Stevie Wonder, Marvin Gaye, Isaac Hayes, and Donny Hathaway were belting out tales about ghetto life. "Gangstas and dope dealers are more entertaining than journalists and professors," the professor reminded me. I could feel my reporter's notebook start to disintegrate from lack of respect. "I think people get entertainment and public relations mixed up," Boyd argued. "Pop culture is about entertainment, and the ghetto is very entertaining. What people refer to as positive images, well, that's about PR and spin. In other words, PR starts with the question: Which image will make the race look the best? Those are two completely different objectives."

As usual, reality-check Dr. B had a point. Author and cultural critic Scott Poulson Bryant goes a step further in his writing, dismissing the need for positive images altogether, instead calling for images that are smart. Maybe my expectations are misplaced. A young reporter once asked me, how as a journalist do you convince someone to talk? (A reporter's notebook is not as tempting as the fifteen minutes that a TV camera can offer, so print journalists can hear a lot of "no comment.") I had never really thought about the nuts and bolts of how I did my job before. The only advice I could come up with was to be fair. I was embarrassed to be passing on such a trite truism. However, I believe most people refuse to talk to a reporter not because they think a story about themselves would turn out bad. Instead I think folks are reluctant to talk because they think the story will come out wrong. Your getting the story wrong is the only way they think they could look bad. Therefore if you convince someone that you will be fair, they will be more likely to open up. Perhaps it is not really positive images that we are yearning for but rather images that are fair. Still, I guess I'm just left wondering (and wishing) when fair . . . or smart . . . or, even, positive images will become entertaining.

Meanwhile, when it comes to ghetto lit, what's ironic about the Souljah turning point is that her novel is a tale of a girl who suffered after refusing to give up her ghetto lifestyle when her drug-dealing pops moves the family to the burbs for a better life. Souljah was not celebrating the lifestyle but criticizing it. She herself is a character in the book who delivers preachy lessons to our ghetto princess. The lesson is clear: holding on to ghetto is not a good thing. But then again, the profit factor has a tendency to water down messages like that. (Sounds a lot like what happened to hip-hop, doesn't it?)

I couldn't stop thinking about any of this—this corporation of hip-hop, this celebrating the worst, this choices thang, and this Bastard named Dirty—when I was eating lunch with Kwame from *The Apprentice*. Most of us with a TV set know who he is, which I realized when, as we ate, strangers kept approaching, wanting to shake his hand and ask what he was doing now. (For the record, Kwame used his fame to launch Legacy Holdings, a real estate development and financial firm with the goal of developing Black wealth and entrepreneurialism in "everything we do.")

While most of us know who Kwame the *Apprentice* star is, how many of us know Kwame Nkrumah, the Ghanaian leader and father of Pan-Africanism for whom Kwame was named? For Ghanaians, missing the reference would be like an American missing a reference to Lincoln or Jefferson in someone's name.

The other thing that anyone with a TV set knows is that Kwame from *The Apprentice* has a Harvard MBA. (Ironically, his book smarts—something a whole generation of Black parents had fought off hoses and dogs for their children to be able to achieve—seemed to be a knock against him in the Trump boardroom at the end of the inaugural season of the reality show. The real estate mogul looked across the table at the well-educated and uncannily poised young Black man and worried that he was all degrees and no experience.)

As Kwame sat down for lunch there was no mention of the "from *The Apprentice*" part of his name, but he instead introduced himself as he is recognized by the state and his mama: Kwame Toure Jackson. "Stokely was named after me," he joked, showing off some of those book smarts. In 1978—four years *after* Kwame was born—Stokely Carmichael, as in the father of Black Power, changed his name to Kwame Toure in acknowledgment of Kwame Nkrumah of Ghana, the father of pan-Africanism, and of the former Guinean president Sékou Touré, first president of an independent African nation. The pairing was also the inspiration for Jackson's parents, or as Kwame describes them, "pseudo-revolutionaries of the sixties, Howard U, March on Washington, Afros, the *movement*" folks. As a student of history, I appreciated the *Apprentice* contestant's joke about his name. As a Black woman obsessed with ghetto, I also appreciated that Kwame Toure Jackson rose to be runner-up on a TV show that captivated 40 million viewers, making his name, and all the history that comes with it, permanently cemented in pop culture and uttered in households across the country.

No matter what his name, though, I have to admit that I liked Kwame before I even met him. The fact that he managed to come across in a reality show as a well-educated, well-spoken, intelligent young Black man who did *not* get angry on camera for fifteen weeks was enough for me. Granted, it may not mean much up against twenty-four hours of, say, BET, which even the always-dancing Ellen DeGeneres reportedly watches constantly,[21] but it was a start (and probably proof that my own standards had gotten lower, since a sighting of a Black man who came across as intelligent on TV was cause for celebration).

Then I was reminded why Kwame Toure Jackson mattered so much in Ghettonation. Again, it has to do with options. The danger when the worst that a community has to offer becomes the mainstream is that other (perhaps more uplifting) realities from that community get ignored. The way ghetto lit is taking over Black fiction or the way that "Drop It Like It's Hot" takes over the album. It is that desperate need for balance that makes Kwame most attractive, and why I will continue to be thankful for those fifteen weeks during which he graced our TV sets. Perhaps it is fitting that a reality-TV star teaches us about the very real need for balance.

Recently Will Smith said something that *again* made me listen. At a press conference for the BET awards, Smith, who was hosting the event, decided to use the mike to blast hip-hop. "The kids that are making these trends, making these songs, don't understand the level of effect that Black Americans have around the world," the Fresh Prince said.[22] Turns out the point hit home for the rapper-turned-movie-star when he was in Africa filming his Oscar-nominated performance for *Ali*. Touring Mozambique, he saw something familiar in the faraway land. It was Tupac Shakur. The slain rapper's name was scrawled across the side of a shack in a tiny Mozambique village. When Smith asked why, the kids all said the same thing: they wanted to be like Tupac. For Smith it was an epiphany. "Yes, there are people who fire guns in the street," he admitted, referring to the favorite topic of much of the radio hits these days. "But there's also doctors who go to work in those areas to feed their children." The most important word Smith used in that moment is "also." What Big Willie is yearning for is balance. And I had hope, for a moment.

● ● ●

Ghetto is never going to be destroyed because it is a part of all of us. Finger-pointing never works. We each live it, to different degrees, every day. How much or how little depends on the choices we make. Maintaining a balance is all we can really hope for. For every ODB let's cross our fingers for a KTJ (Kwame Toure Jackson, of course). Or let's be honest, three KTJs, since what I'm still hoping for is that one day our expectations will actually remain steadfastly high instead of abysmally low.

Still, talk of balance, or rather choices, made me think of that question I never did get an answer to. Why? Why does Pharrell *want* to drop it like it's hot if, as he argues, he can do more? Why does Vickie Stringer *want* to name her publishing house after her former drug ring? Why do women *want* to shake their asses . . . on camera . . . as 50 Cent *wants* to rhyme "Look mama show me how you move it / Nuh-nuuh put ya back into it / Do ya thang like there aint nothin to it. / Shake. Shake. Shake that ass girrrrrrl." And all the rest of the ghetto moments that make me shake, shake my head and ask "Why?"

I don't want to judge, I'm not trying to preach, but rather to deliver an old-fashioned "what-are-you-thinking?" smack upside the head the way grandmama&em used to do.

SMACK.

What are we thinking these days?

Ghetto airs our biggest weakness for the world to see: self-hate. That is how Ghettonation thrives. It is why Rusty Jones opted to become an Ol' Dirty Bastard even if that persona was a myth. If we respected ourselves, ghetto wouldn't have a chance. Realizing that is the hardest part of all. And that desire, the *want* to do the things that make the rest of us wonder just "what are we thinking?" is all our problem.

SMACK.

Truth Is Better Than Fiction.

Real seen and heard moments around Ghettonation:

"I'm not gone never worry 'bout buying this dress, 'cause I'm gone bring it back after I go to this party," said too loud, of course, in a Nordstrom in Chicago.

A young man making a court appearance in downtown Brooklyn topped off his Sunday suit with a black do-rag and a Yankees cap.

A block full of white stretch limos delivered four-year-olds to their Head Start graduation in Baltimore. Little pimp suits complete with hats and canes were spotted on many of the pint-sized graduates.

At one point the tagline for one of the DJs of the local dance (not hip-hop) radio station in New York was "Every lady needs a good man on the side."

At a local strip club in Atlanta, a stripper was seen giving a lap dance while eating a chicken wing.

A "Pimps Up/Hos Down" fashion show was held during homecoming at Howard University.

University of Chicago students hold "Straight thuggin'" parties. Theme parties are popular at the elite school. During the "Straight Thuggin'" party on the overwhelmingly white campus rap music was played and guests were required to come as "ghetto" as possible. One white student wore handcuffs dangling from his wrist as he drank a forty from a brown paper bag.

"Ima dead you," yelled one knucklehead to the other on the corner one night in the Village in Manhattan.

In Philadelphia, a successful interior decorator has a client who shells out bundles to change the look of his gorgeous luxury penthouse constantly. It has been great business for the decorator, who recently found out that his client doesn't own the penthouse but rents it.

Seen and heard during the course of *forty-five minutes* at a local playground in Bed-Stuy, Brooklyn: "Ray Ray! Get the fuck over here," a young mama yelled across the park at her two-year-old. "Are you fuckin' crazy? You better come when you hear me callin' you."

A four-year-old in a black-and-yellow Rocawear sweatsuit, including a matching bandanna tied around his head and a diamond stud in his right ear, rides around the playground in a motorized mini yellow Hummer. Kids push and shove to ride, too, but the child allows only girls to sit in the passenger seat next to him.

At the other end of the playground a mother slaps her toddler, Davante, across the face: "Don't you motherfuckin' cry," she yells. "No one told you to drop your Popsicle."

After eating cookies and an ice cream sandwich and drinking an entire bottle filled with bright red liquid, a toddler stands in the middle of the playground and pees on herself. Although everyone on all the nearby park benches can see and smell the incident, not a single one of the adults responsible for her seems to notice. Or changes her diaper. And no one on the benches says a word.

Forty-five minutes is up.

3

GHETTONATION SPEAKS

Ghetto means that you have been through a lot.
—DANIEL, NINETEEN, BROOKLYN

Daniel Howard* is not typical. He got out. The nineteen-year-old lifted himself up from the Atlantic Terminal projects in Brooklyn and made his way to college. Along the way he also happened to codirect a powerful documentary, *Bullets in the Hood: A Bed-Stuy Story*, about gun violence in my neighborhood.

Daniel stumbled into film, pushed by his mama. Linda Howard, trying to raise her boy into a man on her own, was worried that she was going to lose her son to the street. Nothing specific had happened to indicate that the street was winning. Daniel went to school instead of hanging out on the corner and was not in a gang like most of the boys in his neighborhood. But she says that when you are raising a young Black man in the projects, the street is always a fear. For Daniel, constantly trying to avoid the street had him trapped in his own shell.

---

* Name has *not* been changed. It is about time Daniel—the best of Ghettonation—is recognized.

Small and skinny, he rarely talked or looked people in the eye. "I had to get him into something," his mom said.[1] Truth was, Daniel wasn't into much of anything—bad or good. Ask him about his pre-film days and he barely can remember what he did with his time. "I dunno," he says repeatedly. Avoiding the street takes that much work. "He needed some form of self-expression," his mama pushed. "I just felt that he had so much within him that he needed to get out."[2] So Mrs. Howard pushed a reluctant Daniel into a filmmaking program for "inner-city youth" and the camera they handed him changed his life. *Bullets*, which he directed after two years in the program, won honors at Sundance and became the first film ever made by teenagers eligible for an Academy Award.

Living in Bed-Stuy and writing about "ghetto," I got ahold of *Bullets* early on. Folks automatically assumed it would be a natural fit for me, and an unmarked videotape was slipped my way like payola. The first time I saw the film I did something I never do watching movies: I cried. The reality—our reality—was *that* disturbing. Months after crying over the film as I watched it at home, I went to its debut screening in Brooklyn. The screening was free and Ghettonation turned out in force. Seeing Daniel's movie the second time, I teared up again. Honestly, I've been able to bring myself to watch the short film in its entirety only twice. But the images of our self-destruction will always haunt me.

Bullets opens with Daniel's film partner, Terrence, nineteen, walking through the Louis Armstrong housing projects. Terrence calls these projects home. Others call the stereotypical urban wasteland everything else. "People ask me where I'm from," said Mike, a seventeen-year-old Armstrong resident, nodding his head after watching *Bullets*—the movie—at the Brooklyn screening. "I tell 'em I'm from 'Strong Penitentiary.'" You get the point. Conjure up every worst stereotype you have of project life and you've been to Armstrong.

For most of my life my parents worked in various housing projects around New York City. During the summer when my parents ran out of child-care options, my brother and I would go to work with my dad at the projects in our neighborhood where he worked maintenance. We'd tag along with him on his runs up and down graffiti-filled, drug-infested, piss-stained stairwells (the elevators are usually broken or too dangerous to take) to apartments to make repairs. Once in a while he'd let us play in the project playgrounds with the other kids. Most times, when he thought the playground scene was too rough for us to be out of his sight, my dad would just make us wait for hours in the car parked in the employee parking lot. Although I don't have any Marcy-like big-ups that I can make, the projects are not some faraway world to me but part of my world. And Mike is right, there is something jail-like about them all: poor people trapped in unacceptable living conditions wishing they could get out. These days Armstrong is my neighbor and I pass the complex all the time. And pass it is exactly what I do, usually in my car, as fast as I can ride.

In the opening scene of *Bullets*, Terrence rolls through Armstrong comfortably, with his teenage film crew in tow, asking all the guy-on-the-corner types if they have guns. The endless sea of white Ts, baggy jeans, and black do-rags looks a bit comical in its conformity. Terrence sports the uniform of the corner, too. Within the first five minutes of the film Terrence finds a group of teenagers on the roof who, after patting him down to make sure this stranger asking questions is not 5-o, take him to an apartment to show him what they got. In a tiny bedroom with music posters and photographs on the wall (looking like so many rooms I had seen on runs with my dad), one teen lifts up his mattress for the camera to capture a war's worth of weaponry. Clutching one of his guns and taking a drag on a cigarette, the teen admits to shooting someone a few years back. "Did you kill him?" asks Terrence. "Nah," he puffs, "I paralyzed his dumb ass." The young audience at the screening instantly started to laugh. I wish they hadn't. On screen the show-and-tell teen boasts that the biggest gun in the pile—some kind of action-movie Uzi—was a gift from his father. These man-boys are not typical either. I hope.

Still, that wasn't even the worst part. Without warning, one of the teens pulls out a revolver from the exposed waistband of his colorful boxers and points the gun directly at the camera. "A gun can make anyone do anything," he says with so much bass in his voice that the words almost sounds like a club hit.

He then pulls the trigger.

Daniel was behind the camera.

Judging by the steady camera shot, he *didn't* flinch. Judging by the slight glimmer of stunned fear that flashes across Terrence's face on screen, it is obvious that neither budding filmmaker knew that the gun was *not* loaded. It was the only time I've ever come close to looking into the barrel of a real gun. The camera may not have jumped, but I did— heading straight to the ladies room at the first click of the trigger.

After seeing this scene I had to meet Daniel. He didn't disappoint. When our paths crossed he was home in Brooklyn for the summer after finishing his first year of college. I've always felt that the first summer home is an interesting time for those who get out. It is when you see your old world and your new world collide. The crash can be overwhelming.

I worked two jobs that first summer back after my Ivy League vacation. Not internships, or career-building experiences, no résumé listings, but jobs. (Theme song: Donna Summer's "She Works Hard for the Money" is too easy, try Jay-Z's fitting "Hard Knock Life" [Ghetto Anthem].) They were the last jobs I've ever worked.

During the day I was a salesgirl in the same local clothing store where I worked during high school. This time I was one of the full-timers, though, something I had vowed never to become. It meant ten-hour shifts six days a week, and forced overtime, all on your feet. The can-I-help-you? smile I was required to sport all day was enough to drive me insane.

When I was done at the store, I walked the streets as a census taker. The response to the 1990 census was so poor in neighborhoods like mine that the government was hiring folks to go door-to-door to count the uncounted. Taking the census meant knocking on some of the most unsavory doors. These were people who generally did not care about being counted by the U.S. government for whatever reason. Their most common reaction was to slam their door in my face. I visited drug fronts, *slam*. Illicit love dens, *slam*. Shooting galleries, *slam*. Illegal-immigrant holding pens, *slam*. And families living so far below the line that answering the census form could rightfully never be on their list of things to do, *slam*. It made my salesgirl gig seem like a dream job.

Between the jobs and looking at my neighborhood through college-opened eyes, for the first time I was learning lessons on what it was like to be a straddler. Those who get out of the ghetto often can continue to understand and identify with that mind-set while still rejecting it as their world expands. It becomes easy, almost natural, to slip in and out of the mind-set, too. Wearing different masks where appropriate is part of survival. I learned more that summer about myself and ourselves than ever before. I was proud of where I was from. Those corners are a part of me and helped make me who I am. My creativity comes from always trying to expand my world beyond my small little apartment. Any toughness that I have comes from always staying close to my brother even if it meant I was the only girl on a playground full of boys. I have smarts from the streets that have carried me far. And I am not afraid—of the unknown, of tomorrow, of life—because of where I'm from. Those corners—filled with folks who were (or should be) thankful to be alive—taught me to cherish life. (Or end up on the corner.) Most important, though, being back home on the corner, working that summer peeking behind people's doors, living in a world far away from the courtyards of my college campus, taught me that, yes, there are lines. But no matter what side we stand on, we are not as different from those on the other side of the line as we think we are.

Daniel was showing signs of the straddler pull, too. In addition to earning a four-year scholarship to a college in South Carolina, he had also snagged a coveted internship at the NBC affiliate down there for the summer. However, he still firmly held on to his Brooklyn roots ("I don't live in South Carolina," he corrected me, despite the four years he will be there, if all goes well. "I just go to school there!") even as he expressed frustration that when he's back home too many of his peers do not want to see beyond Brooklyn ("Brooklyn is *not* the world.") Overall, though, he seemed to be handling the collision well.

Before we could even sit down he was overflowing with nervous chatter about social ills, music, politics, and BML (Black Man Life) Whatisms. BML Whatisms are those facts-of-life conclusions that Black men come to by living their life as Black men. It can be something subtle like never sitting with your back to the door in a restaurant. Or something more substantial, like knowing that as a Black man, when the you-know-what hits the fan, you are the first suspect. (A BWL Whatism? In the pyramid of office respect, the understanding that she will always be at the very bottom, below white men, Black men, and white women. No matter what, carrying the baggage of race and gender—not to mention that big chip on our shoulders that everyone is convinced will be there before we walk into a room—guarantees that Black women sink to the bottom of the pyramid.)

It didn't take long before this nugget rolled off Daniel's tongue: "I feel a lot of young Black men my age are still trying to find who they are," he began. I scooted up my chair ready and eager for the BML Whatism to follow. "For most people the definition of young Black males is someone who is a thug, wearing baggy pants, high-top sneakers, fitted hat. It needs to change. If we don't change it, we are going to be stuck in this vertigo where we don't know who we are," he ended. "That is how I feel," he added, after a pause, as if to make his point less important. (This flash of unnecessary lack of confidence reminded me of the way women in the office tend to "uptalk" or raise their voice an octave at the end of their sentences as if they are asking a question even when they are making a declarative statement. Such self-sabotage should be called what it is—ghetto.) Still, "how Daniel feels" is significant. It seems he found eyes-wide-open enlightenment off at college. I wondered what that will mean for the thought police. Bad news, I hope. Par-tay!

I wasn't sure yet how this idea of self-discovery fit into why things are so ghetto these days, but it struck me. It seemed that we were indeed experiencing this vertigo, as Daniel described. "The hardest part about being young and Black?" he said, repeating my question as he thought. "The hardest part? Honestly? It is showing people that you are not the American Black man but the Black man who knows who he is and knows himself. It is easier to fit in the stereotype than be what you think a Black man should be."

Daniel is referring to low expectations in action.

Hearing Daniel talking about the hardest part about being a Black man got my reporter's juices flowing. I wanted to know why? Why now? Stereotypes and negativity have always existed, why are they celebrated now? That is, after all, what makes all this ghetto. The eyes-wide-open Daniel, with his new college student juices flowing, had just one answer: the media.

Out of the back pocket—of his baggy jeans—he pulled a well-read, aging copy of *The Assassination of the Black Male Image* by Earl Ofari Hutchinson and slid it across the table as if breaking me off a piece of that fresh knowledge he was swimming in. Hutchinson, a prolific author and social commentator, came of age during the civil rights and Black Power movements. A race man, he was not afraid to call Black, Black, by any means necessary. He earned a warm spot in my heart when he became one of the very few high-profile Black faces to publicly protest the NAACP's decision to nominate R. Kelly for an Image award *after* the singer had already been charged with child pornography in the wake of the discovery of a smutty video of him allegedly having sex with a fourteen-year-old girl. Hutchinson was one of too few high-profile Black faces to see that publicly recognizing the likes of R. Kelly just wasn't right, thereby proving his willingness to stand strong alone, while the rest of us willingly sit contently together in our ghetto way. (Let's face it, even without the twenty-one-count indictment and piss-stained bedsheets, should the nation's premier civil rights organization *ever* be honoring someone responsible for making "Feelin' on yo booty" and "You remind me of my jeep" catchphrases of an era?)

"In the media, in the videos, all you see is the illest cycle of us being portrayed," said Daniel, faithful to the Hutchinson school. "We are someone who is supposed to be violent, someone who is supposed to talk a certain way, the Bling Bling. There is a lot of media brainwashing going on," he said. "But it is okay to be who you are," he adds, this time without any "how-I-feel" qualification.

Some things you just know without needing convincing, explanation, or even proof. These are the little ingrained things in life you take for granted. Like no one will be able to cook your favorite meal better than Mom. Or your child is always the smartest, cutest, most talented in any room. Or Lil' Jon is ghetto. The list may be different for everyone, except the Lil' Jon part—he's just ghetto—always. Add to my list of knowisms: always being true to yourself. Life is not worth the hardships if you are not going to "be who you are." Not embracing yourself is a vulnerability that is too easy to exploit. I am proud to be a Black woman, period. It is who I am and how I live my life. I can never forget, disrespect, or devalue that. Especially when there are too many out there who are eager to do it for me. That is why Daniel's "be who you are" conclusion was like the best Mom-made comfort food for me. And I was beginning to think there weren't too many of us out there capable of enjoying such a dish.

During all my conversations on corners with young people from around the way what I found most troubling was how fuzzy we are about success. Ask someone what the meaning of ghetto is and usually they are eager to spit out some kind of disturbing scenario in disgust. Ask what it means to be successful and you are likely to encounter an uncomfortably long pause. This is what happened when I started asking this question of teenagers in my ghetto, Bed-Stuy. It happened on the urban corners of Brooklyn, suburban corners of Long Island, and bourgie corners of Atlanta. It happened in Cleveland, in Baltimore, in D.C. It happened in Dallas, San Diego, and Oakland. It happened in Chicago, North Carolina, New Jersey, and Connecticut. Mention success and over and over again I would get back the blank stare. Even for those who could eventually muster an answer—either with prodding or on their own—it was after first giving me the blank stare. The stereotype is winning.

Aisha is a gawky entanglement of long, taut runner's limbs that always seem to be in motion, even when she is sitting still. One day when she grows a little confidence and gets some meat on her bones she will be drop-dead stunning. Today she has just turned eighteen and is bursting with potential. Aisha lives in an apartment in Bed-Stuy with two parents, each of whom has some college, and both work good jobs for the city. Her older sister got out and is now a mother and married to a man "who works in a bank." Aisha goes to a Catholic school outside of Bed-Stuy, not for the morning prayer, but for the discipline and education that her parents think a place like Bed-Stuy's local public school, Boys and Girls High, their alma mater, can't provide. The teenager's afternoons are spent not on the corner but at either track or basketball practice for the school and private leagues around Brooklyn that her parents keep her busy with. In a couple of months she will be out of Brooklyn and off to college at a school in the Midwest. Unlike many of the teens I've talked to, Aisha is convinced that her family is "very successful." It is. Ask her what she is most proud of and she is quick to answer how she managed to "stay focused." She did. By anyone's standards Aisha is a good kid. The type who always makes eye contact when she says "Good afternoon" on her way home from school and who insists on addressing me as Mrs., which is more manners than I see from the majority of people in my neighborhood. Yet when we start to sit down and talk about all things ghetto, I am still struck by how little she knows about what success means. She is, however, quick to say that her family is "very successful." That is more than I can get from the likes of Chris, sixteen, who could not point to a single person in his world he considered to be successful. The closest was a distant uncle he had met maybe once who still lived in the DR (Dominican Republic) and ran a hotel or an apartment building or a baseball team or knew the DR president or something along those lines. Terrence, on the other hand, tried to brush off my question about success completely as if he was too bored or busy to even discuss it, the way teenagers do when they don't want to think about something. He did make sure to give the respectful answer and offer up his mama as successful. But, again, he couldn't tell me why except that she was his mama.

Aisha was different, though, because she is indeed very focused. Getting to college has been what she has worked toward for years now, and why she is an outsider and an insider, a straddler, in our neighborhood. Yet even though she generally defines success in professional terms, she didn't seem to know what any of the "successful" members of her family did for a living that made them so successful. In fact, I knew more about the careers of her family members (a nurse, a transit clerk, a mid-level manager) from idle neighborhood chitchat than she did. In her mind, her brother-in-law is the most successful because he "works in a bank," but she has absolutely no idea what he does at the bank. (He doesn't actually work at a branch bank, but is a mid-level manager at a Fortune 500 financial services and banking company's corporate headquarters.)

I don't think there is just a single answer to the success question. I tend to think that living a successful life has to do with not limiting your possibilities. The meaning of success constantly grows and develops, changing from person to person, and from generation to generation. Defining success should be difficult. However, what worried me about my discussions on the corner was that, for the young people I interviewed, not only was coming up with a definition difficult, but their lack of details indicated that the idea of being successful was like imagining something out of this world, or out of their world.

If our young people do not have a clear vision of what it means to them to be successful, then how can we expect them to ever get there?

Now, I was beginning to understand where the lack of hope comes from. (Us?) Could it be? (Us?) And I wasn't liking my realization. (Us?) This was becoming a journey I began to wish I had never made. This "no-low" (no hopes, low expectations) combination is the foundation of ghetto. It is what drives that man-boy back at the Louis Armstrong projects to pull the trigger of a gun in the face of the camera. And since his gun was pointed at us, it also means that the devastating "no-low" isn't just his problem, but ours.

"There is a lot of things going on in our communities. . . ." Mrs. Clayburne started to say. She should know. Her nineteen-year-old son, Timothy, was shot and killed by a police officer on the roof of the Louis Armstrong projects. Terrence was standing directly behind Timothy on the roof that day. The force of the bullet sent the two best friends — one alive, one dying — tumbling down a flight of stairs. The NYC police commissioner later called the shooting "unjustified." The tragedy became the focus of *Bullets*.

Mrs. Clayburne is a local crossing guard. She works out of the same police precinct as the cop who killed her son. It means she sees him all the time. She is still the type of woman who calls strangers "sweetheart" and "baby" even though she now has a bitterness in her heart. Since her son's death she has trouble sleeping. She's smoking again, too, after six years of not picking up a cigarette. Her days are filled with "prayer and protest." It was the twenty-fourth night of January when Tim-Tim, as his mother calls him, was gunned down. On the twenty-fourth of every month since, Mrs. Clayburne holds a vigil for her son. At first the neighborhood turned out in force for the monthly vigil. These days she is the only one guaranteed to be there with candle in hand. "My God sits on a high throne," she said. "And He will have the last say."[3] Meanwhile, this mother was so consumed with the loss of her son that she didn't notice that she was starting to lose her daughter. After the shooting, her daughter, Timetress (pronounced *tih-MEE-truss*; the children's father is named Timothy) dropped out of community college. Her plan was to get pregnant. She hadn't told her family or even her boyfriend about her master plan, but with her paychecks from Starbucks she started stocking up on baby clothes and toys. "I just want someone to love me like my brother did," she said, "and my baby will."[4]

Through the years I had seen Mrs. Clayburne with her STOP sign protecting my neighborhood's children cross the street. But I never knew all the "things going on" in her community before the night I met Daniel. "There is a lot of things going on in our communities," Mrs. Clayburne said, "and the only one who can make a change is us. We have to start pulling *ourselves* together."

Which brings us back to Daniel and his understandable rant against the Media. Because I am a member of the Media, my gut won't honestly let me argue that there is not indeed a Dark Side. But since Mrs. Clayburne had my back with her make-a-change-ourselves urgings, I had to push further. Even with the Dark Side, there's still choice. I asked Daniel, the budding filmmaker, about music videos since he was the one who had uttered "in the media, in the videos" in the same breath. We chatted about Lil' Kim and Young Jeezy, and 50 Cent, *just a li'l bit*. You could almost see the gears of his young mind cranking as he began to work out and develop his thoughts right before my eyes. "It is like we're, we're"—he pauses as the cranks click—"we're bashing ourselves!" Lightbulb! "But the media are the gatekeepers." Exactly. "They allow what gets out." Exactly. By this point his frustration was building as his thoughts took him from one logical stop to the next. "And right now the gatekeepers are taking a look at us like we are a bunch of monkeys." E-xact-ly. "It is like a jail that we are locked in. Someone needs to take the initiative and get the keys."

Gail is a mother of a five-year-old. We are exactly the same age. She works for the city just like my parents did. When I talk to her, I sometimes feel like she is a mixture of their worlds and mine. I enjoy the bridge. Gail was walking home from work one day with her son when the gunplay started. Gunplay is actually the most appropriate description I can think of since the two wielding the guns were no more than twelve years old. The corner was one of the gentrified corners of my supposedly quickly changing Bed-Stuy. Houses on that corner have doubled and tripled in price in the last three years. Young white professionals pour past that corner every day without seeing the old guards sitting on the stoops, the next generation playing in the street, the last generation watching from their windowsills, and the mothers, like Gail. As always, the gunplay that day started without warning. *They shootin'!* Gail's son was a few steps in front of her, busily playing kick the can, when *she looked.* The two boys with the guns were shooting at each other directly over her son's head. Without hesitation she smacked the shooter's hand nearest her again and again and with the spanking forced his gun to point to the sky. "If their parents don't care," she said through tears triggered by telling me her worst memory, "then I have got to do something."

Her expectations are higher. The boys stopped shooting. And I wickedly smiled, thinking, if only she had a belt.

In all seriousness, though, Gail and Mrs. Clayburne aren't the only ones stuck on what we can do ourselves. It is something I heard over and over again as I stood on the corners in my journeys. "If you don't take control of your life," said Bama, so called because his people are from Alabama, as he stood on a corner in Bed-Stuy, "people will be happy to see you die—in Iraq, down South, or here in Brooklyn." Bama is one of the hey-baby guys I see on the corner every morning on my way to work. I wasn't really sure how Bama was adhering to his own advice on taking control of life since I see him morning and evening on the same corner every day. This particular evening he was missing the pair of square diamonds that usually pull down his earlobes, and he was dressed in a baby blue tracksuit with orange trim. The head-to-toe color scheme was noticeably subdued for Bama, and probably why I was able to chat with him that night with a (somewhat) straight face. The first time we spoke almost a year before I was blinded by all the sunshine yellow he was sporting—T, cap, sneakers, and tracksuit. I soon discovered that his always new and pressed tracksuits seem to come in every Lucky Charms color. The baby blue one is my favorite. (I be ghetto.) Still, regardless of his rainbow worship, I was pleasantly surprised by his insightful BML Whatism. Because, "people will be happy to see you die." Point.

The blank stares about success bothered me more than I expected. They weighed on my mind for weeks because all I could think was that they were a sign that we have failed. "Failed at what?" my husband demanded to know. Failed(!), I thought to myself. Failed at the big picture, the game of life, the struggle to move onward and upward. Failed at what counts, what matters. Faced with my thoughts, all I could muster to answer was the one word: "failed," I whispered.

It then sank in how much we must not be passing on our stories, our history, ourselves. As a Black journalist who has spent much of my career trying to make our voices heard, I took this failure personally. "I don't know that historical apathy is any worse now than it's been, honestly, but people think that it is," said Dr. B, trying to ease my worst fears. "If you get past the bullshit, what is really going on is that this generation [grown folks, civil rights intelligentsia, powers that be folks, babyboomers, my parents, his generation] is passing *into* history, but they don't want to go and so they chide the next generation for not knowing their history."

Hmmm. The journalist in me hoped Dr. B is right about that. The Black in me felt guilty. It means too many of us are not doing our part.

One day during one of our conversations, Daniel stumbled down this road of thought: "So not only do we have white people stereotyping us but sometimes we have our own Black folks stereotyping us as well," he said. (Are your ears burning?) "It is like there is a class system, a border between Black professionals and poor Black people that needs to be broken."

In an instant I felt my "older and thus wiser" badge slip off. (Such honors are always debatable, anyway. But, like a necessary chaser, sometimes you need something to wash down the old part.) Now I was the one who found myself caught in a blank stare of silence as Daniel's words rang in my ears. I had heard the frustration, the resentment, the anger before—in one way or another—on corner after corner in my ghetto journeys. It was just as strong as the wagging fingers from my usual "day crowd" of professionals. Indeed, Daniel was right. And I was, just, older.

"They," said Mary Pattillo, a sociologist at Northwestern who studies the Black middle class. "They surely want to change the behavior of the poor, Black people who live there."[5] Pattillo's latest research is on gentrification, specifically of Black neighborhoods being gentrified not by moneyed white folks but by moneyed Black folks. The "they" in this case are Black professionals moving back to the, well, ghetto. Unfortunately, when the two worlds collide, there ends up being a lot of tsk-tsking going on.

Pattillo's forthcoming book, *Black on the Block: The Politics of Race and Class in the City*, is based on five years of research in which she examined Black neighborhoods in Chicago, where the city is replacing public housing projects with market-rate town houses and condos. The

Chicago Housing Authority is in the process of demolishing 15,000 public housing units with the hopes of raising property values by scattering low-income residents across the city. Mayor Richard Daley has touted the plan as a way to support and build the middle class. Pattillo is intrigued by the fragility of class among Black folks. She suggests that because the Black middle class is more likely than the white middle class to come from poor families and to have poor siblings, fragility is embedded in its networks. The housing shake-up in Chicago provides a perfect lab to observe how these layers interact. Namely, can there be a (Black) community in a mixed-income neighborhood, or does the class thing get in the way?

Pattillo's research into the gentrification of the South Side of Chicago resonates with what Daniel fears. It seems in these ghetto times that too many of us are weighed down by a "we are better than you" chip on our shoulders. "At the end of my block, it's like a total other world," said Linda, one of the bourgie gentrifiers. Linda and her husband Mike, an economist, built a new house in the Bronzeville section of Chicago's South Side on newly cleared land that used to be the site of towering public housing projects. "I hate to say this because these are my people. But this is just a different world for us. If there weren't people like my husband and me moving into neighborhoods like Bronzeville, they would continue to decline." Linda and Mike do not feel any remorse about the folks who were displaced when the projects came tumbling down because "that's not appropriate housing for anybody." "The people who would disagree," added Mike, wearing an I ♥ BLACK PEOPLE T-shirt, "are the people who grew up there and don't know any better."[6] I don't know how to brush the chip off Mike's shoulder.

That border that Daniel is talking about, that gap—mental and physical—between the classes that we are living with now, that is what is killing us, softly. (Well, in some cases quite harshly.) In the end, no matter what rung on the ladder we may be on, everyone needs balance. Such balance can serve as a constant reminder of the possibilities upward or downward. Without it both classes will remain trapped in the ghetto—the mind-set.

By the end of my journeys, one thing was clear, Ghettonation had a lot to say. Their wants are simple, really. The people want to be heard. Santos, a sixteen-year-old with acne-stained cheeks and personality to spare, claims his favorite teacher is Mrs. Grimes "because she listens." "She remembers everything you tell her," said Santos, who, like Chris or Terrence or most teenage boys, is talkative only when prodded. Not knowing Mrs. Grimes or what goes on in her classroom in Bushwick, a rougher part of Brooklyn than Bed-Stuy, I find it almost startling that something as basic as just remembering what Santos has to say could place this teacher at the top of his list of favorites. This young voice is really not demanding that much.

After months of listening, I had to admit I wasn't sure that I was any further along in my quest for the Answer than when I started. We started with the identity crisis, moved to the media's role in creating that crisis, jumped to our own responsibility, and ended with a self-destructive class divide.

"We are not a lost cause," Daniel said defiantly, snapping me out of my own no-hope daze. "When a lot of people think of young Black youth they think we are a lost cause, that there is no way we can break out. But that's not true. I'm breaking out of it, and it would be nice to have some help on this end."

$$$

Blowing a paycheck in a weekend.

Taking pride in being broke ("I'm broker than a mofo," said loud and proud).

Using the last bit of money in your pocket for anything but rent, food, bills.

Having your phones, including cellies, shut off every other month because the bill is not paid.

Subscribing to the "get rich or die trying" mantra. What about put it in the bank or die broke?

Flashing money you don't have instead of making your money last. (Hip-hop is a platinum and diamond mine of "broker than a mofo" celebrities living on record-label credit and borrowed gear.)

4 PLEASE, BABY, PLEASE

*Ghetto journey entry # 69: Pssssst, Maaaaaaa, God
bless your smile. You're beautiful, you know that? What's
your name, baby? C'mon, you can tell me your name. I
just want to be friends. You think we can be friends?
Here's my number. You gonna call me? Please, baby,
baby, please.*

It was the summer of Usher—2004—and there was
no escaping the sounds of his best-selling album
Confessions. An album on which the chorus of the
title track nonchalantly croons: "Just when I
thought I said all I can say / My chick on the side
said she got one on the way / These are my confessions"—all to a phat bounce-your-head beat, of
course. As someone whose musical tastes are
driven by that bounce-your-head beat meter, I
never thought I'd miss an old-fashioned love song.
But after hearing my husband—who treats the car
as if it is his own soundproof recording studio—
sing along with Usher's chorus for the umpteenth
time that summer, I couldn't stop missing.

Babydaddies, shorty, wifey, on-the-side—I don't get any of it, thank-fully. We all find ourselves in positions that may be far from ideal. That's what life is. But now on-the-side has become an official category of relationship. Where once upon a time these situations were consid-ered shameful and used to be chalked up to "I had no choice" desire, "It just happened" circumstance, or even "It didn't mean anything" ar-rogance, these days so many of these "relationships" have become a choice—even the first choice. Ghetto.

Pssssssst, hey ma . . .

I started to realize how far the mind-set had spread the moment I be-gan wearing a wedding ring. Almost instantly the men came knock-ing—on the subway, at the office, on the street. I am no fool; the offers had nothing to do with me. I was the exact same person the day before my wedding as the day after. It was just that now I had that magic glow of unattainability, which makes my value in the ghetto love book sky-rocket. So when I tell these dogs-in-heat that I'm a married woman, they see it as the ultimate challenge, the beginning of their fight instead of the end.

The other important draw about that gold band is the commitment factor, or rather the lack-of-commitment factor. A married woman, or anyone who is already attached to someone else, is seen as less work be-cause all the relationship responsibilities already fall on someone else's shoulders. Think of it as the difference between how we treat a part-time job and a career. Part-time jobs typically do not provide us with benefits, vacation time, health insurance, or overtime, so why should we invest more than the minimum—completing just the hours paid for? The goal is the check, necessary to make ends meet. You don't go beyond the call of duty for a part-time job; there is no long-term invest-ment. Which is different from a career, where supposedly investing in longtime growth—putting in time, effort, dedication—is necessary for the biggest payoffs. By definition, a relationship with someone *else's* partner is a part-time commitment. And thus this kind of gig is nothing more than a way of helping make ends meet. Expectations, complaints, emotional involvement—all are kept to a minimum, leaving the fun factor at a maximum. There is no reason to get involved with bad moods, unexpected hardships, basic problems, or even dependability. If you get to see someone only a few days a week, a month, or a year then why argue? Why go grocery shopping? Why look a mess? There is no reason to do a lot of work when you can still reap the benefits. So, instead, you laugh, you eat out; you look fly—always—and you get it on (even if you have a headache) because there might not be a next time. Up against the difficulty of the real world, on-the-side can seem like a wonderful vacation. Thus it is the ideal situation for someone who does not have the maturity to take on the responsibilities of a real relationship. That's what makes it ghetto.

But true partnership takes time, relationships involve baggage, and just like life, sometimes it is not always fun.

Psssssst, hey baby . . .

One of the security guards at my job always used to say hello in the morning. Nothing more, nothing less. I come from a household where not acknowledging familiar faces with a hello was the ultimate crime, so the ritual didn't really stand out for me. Then one Monday Mr. Security Guard gave me something more. He added to his hello that he had seen me on the subway over the weekend. I remembered the trip; it was Christmas season and my husband and I were bogged down with bags, struggling with our load and desperately hoping for a pair of seats on the train as we headed home to Bed-Stuy. It turns out the security guard and I live only a few blocks from each other—me with my husband and he with his mom. Immediately for me the scenario felt a little awkward because I couldn't understand why someone who says

"Hi" every day of the week would deliberately let it be known that he did *not* say "Hi" on Saturday. Then he mentioned that he had seen that I was with my boyfriend—husband, I corrected him—and the conversation pretty much ended. The next time he spoke, about a week or so later, he asked me out. I was a bit stunned. Why would a man who saw me every day ask me out on a date only *after* he found out I was married? Because on-the-side was his choice. And that is sad.

It doesn't matter what we tell ourselves about making such a choice. Whether it is the desperate "he's/she's worth it" mantra. (I have a single friend who had a decade-long affair with a married man that survived that long because "he's the one" and, "he'll leave her." He wasn't and he never did.) Or the empowering: "All the fun, none of the work" slogan. (That was Mr. Security Guard's motivation, he later admitted.) Or even the illogical I'm "The Man/Badass Chick" excuses that we tell ourselves if we are able to make someone else's partner stray. It doesn't take a Dr. Love PhD to see that being thrilled over getting someone's partner to stray is not really proof of your own irresistibility but instead proof of your own run-of-the-mill insecurities, your need for such an over-the-top ego stroking to help you feel like The Man/Badass Chick.

Truth is, we all have weak moments. No one is perfect. But the reality is, to *choose* the on-the-side role, to willingly put yourself in such a second-class status, means that what you expect *and* accept for yourself is pretty low. It is like returning to the back of the bus. If you don't think you deserve anything better, then why should anyone else?

Psssst, hey ma . . .

It is hard to determine when the bar got so low—for both genders. In fact, the biggest mistake we make is thinking that the on-the-side mentality is a sickness that strikes just women with low self-esteem. Besides the afternoon talk-show circuit that tells us so, there are also books, newsletters, discussion groups, tests—as in the Ultimate Self-esteem Test—and even Web sites, including selfesteem4women.com and the blunt moreselfesteem.com, devoted to the myth. But there are lots of Mr. Security Guards out there, too. Such an epidemic makes it hard to determine when the bar got so low, but that summer of Usher sure seemed a good moment to go "hmmmmmm." Arsenio-style, of course.

Because of its naughty-boy exploits (the CD *is* called *Confessions*), Usher's CD sold 1.1 million its first week, making it the biggest debut ever by an R&B artist and causing just as much gossipy buzz over whether the confessions were actually true. Usher coyly kept people guessing, and all the talk will surely be chalked up as one of those pointless less filling/tastes great debates as to whether sales were helped more if such confessions were true or not. By the end of the year the CD had sold almost 8 million copies in the United States (13 million worldwide), more than the combined sales for the number two (Norah Jones) and number three (Eminem) CDs that year. In fact, the Grammy award–winning album of on-the-side lyricism is just shy of joining Michael Jackson's *Thriller*, the Beatles' *Sgt. Pepper's Lonely Hearts Club Band*, Prince's *Purple Rain*, Pink Floyd's *The Wall*, and Outkast's *Speakerboxxx/The Love Below* on the list of the best-selling albums of all time.[1] Which means the reach of that on-the-side message is staggering.

It's not just music, though. Reality TV shows have also followed suit. Once upon a time we had a show called *The Dating Game* where the goal was to interview (yes, talk to) three potential suitors in order to choose the best date. With its dirty innuendos, the campy, over-the-top show was still dripping with the sexuality that we are used to today, but it was all words and the curtain divide stopped things from turning into an orgy. Today we have something like *The Bachelor*, which is, basically, the sanctioned adventures of a player. The nation watches as one man dates dozens of women at the same time and then tries to make it romantic by offering a single red rose and jewelry. It's a big leap from sex talk to pimp walk.

In 2005 one of the most celebrated independent films was *Hustle & Flow*, a movie about a pimp-turned-rapper in Memphis. The film earned Terrence Howard an Oscar nomination for playing the pimp, who we are supposed to care about because, I guess, a white boy raised in California wrote and directed every degrading word that came out of the Black cast's mouths. At one point in the film, this hero of the new age kicks one of his hos—and her screaming baby—out of his house in the middle of the night because she has the nerve to call him a bitch, or rather a "motherfucking bitch." The climax of the movie, just like winning the championship in a clichéd sports flick, is the pimp's music hit. The pimp's big song? "Beat That Bitch," the name of which was quickly changed to "Whomp That Trick" for radio airplay. How lovely. For the record, there was no way I was going to increase box office revenue by going to see such degrading trash. (I had a bad feeling about the film from the very first preview, the way you get a bad feeling when served a tray of fish on an airplane. Sometimes you just know.) Instead I gave *H&F* the respect that it was worth and bought a $5 bootleg copy at the fried fish joint near my house. It allowed me the pleasure to rant and rave at what did prove to be degrading trash in the comfort of my own bedroom while munching on a damn good samich. (I be ghetto.)

Pssst, hey baby . . .

Usher, reality TV, trashy movies, does any of this matter? It is natural to think no. (And believe me, I'd much rather exist in a world where Usher, reality TV, and trashy movies definitely don't matter.) Let's be honest, pop culture isn't that creative. Instead it is inherently reactive. With profit always the goal, there is only one rule: give the people what they want. What is created is governed, controlled, even driven by the rule, which is used as the reason, excuse, and explanation of every decision. (It is what allows folks like "not my responsibility" Pharrell to keep their heads up.)

Too often we fall in the trap of holding pop culture up as a window on reality. The assumption is that somehow movies, music, TV give us a window into a moment. I tend to think that the profit motive distorts that view, though. Pop culture isn't really a window on how we are actually living. Instead it is a reflection of what is going on in our minds, our mood. It is our mind-set. Pop culture portrays how we wish we were living, think we should be living, or assume others are living. It is the life stories—fact and fiction—that we expect will be the most, well, popular. And that is why it matters.

Given all of that, what does pop culture say about our wishes, thoughts, and assumptions? What does it say about our mind-set that when it comes to our love lives, typically, these creations are completely dysfunctional, filled with betrayal, disrespect, and low hopes? What does it say that this is what can make a profit, dollars, bank, chedda, paper? At the least, it says "we so ghetto."

A recent study published in the *American Journal of Public Health* tried to link rap music to sexual behavior. Researchers from Emory University studied Black teenage girls ages fourteen to eighteen who watched an average of twenty-one hours of videos a week. Of course, any teenager who has the time to watch that much unsupervised TV is vulnerable to rolling downhill. . . . Still, the results, which were adjusted for family income and one- or two-parent households, are hard to ignore. Researchers found that over a twelve-month period the girls hooked on videos were twice as likely to have multiple sexual partners as those who were not watching as much. The video watchers were also 1.5 times more likely to have acquired an STD, used drugs, and used alcohol. During the twelve-month period, 15 percent of the girls under study had sexual intercourse with someone other than their steady partner and almost 38 percent acquired an STD. If girls watched more than twenty-one hours a week, the chances that they contracted an STD that year jumped to 60 percent, and they were 60 percent more likely to use alcohol and drugs.[2]

"The harm is it affects your perception of the world," says one of the authors of the study, Dr. Ralph DiClemente of Emory, about videos. "Is a relationship acceptable if my partner curses at me? Emotionally abuses me? Physically abuses me? Is that acceptable? Well, in rap music videos it is."[3] Pop culture is saying a lot, then.

Psssst, hey ma . . .

In California, law enforcement has been battling what the beat cops call "tennis shoe pimps." That would be teenage boys pimping out girls in their class. They convince the girls to sell sex to classmates or older men for money and clothes, and all share in the wealth. The "tennis shoe" nickname stuck because often these boys, some as young as thirteen or fourteen, usually don't even have their driver's licenses yet. The girls can be as young as twelve, cops say, and often don't see their ho-ing as prostitution but "survival sex" because it is the best way they can see to get the important things they need to survive their lives as teenagers: money for clothes, cosmetics, concerts, and movies.[4] "Teens are pimping teens in Oakland," a member of the Alameda County Task Force devoted to combating the problem told a stunned audience of neighbors and local officials at an East Oakland Crime Prevention Council Meeting.

Unfortunately, tennis shoe pimps are a trend that law enforcement warns is starting to spread across the country. With pimps and players glorified in popular culture, these teenagers think the lifestyle is glamorous and don't see it as being as dangerous as selling drugs. Teachers have reported incidents in some high schools in which they have had to chastise students for bragging about being pimps and hos, even showing off stacks of $100 bills in one San Diego school.

The ugly truth is that underage prostitution has been skyrocketing across the country, with the ages getting younger. In the 1980s the underage sex trade was dominated by runaways caught up in a world of drugs and homelessness and trying to survive. But things have shifted. The fourteen-, fifteen-, sixteen-year-olds selling sex today are different, police say. "They are out there for reasons completely opposite what it was fifteen years ago," says Laura McGowan, a vice detective in San Diego. "They're doing it so they can buy clothes and jewelry and CDs and Walkmen. When you ask them why they are out there, they say they want 'stuff.' "[5]

This behavior cuts across class lines. (San Diego doesn't really conjure up images of rampant hard knocks.) In fact, outreach experts say they are more often working with girls from middle-class and upper-class homes who decided that it would be empowering to sell sex for money.[6] Empowering? No. Ghetto? Yes.

In Oakland the special task force wants to start a public awareness campaign that "counters the glamorization of pimping."[7] But we are living in a world where MTV's *Pimp My Ride* is one of cable's top-rated shows. In a world where 50 Cent's "P.I.M.P" can hit the top of the charts. In a world where Nelly's Pimp Juice Energy Drink rakes in $10 million a year. Megastar Britney Spears capped off her wedding (the second one) by standing by new hubbie, Kevin Federline, and his boys sporting white tracksuits emblazoned with PIMP across their backs to pose for *People* magazine. Even something as innocuous as TV's *Hollywood Squares* is produced by a company called One Ho Productions (founded by center square Whoopi Goldberg). And a world where you can even buy "pimp" and "ho" Halloween costumes for the entire family—mom, dad, teenagers, children (starting at size 4!), and dogs. (Sales of the pimp Halloween line have been so good at brandsonsale.com that the online costume retailer has pledged to get an infant pimp costume out before too long.)[8] In a ghetto world like this, can the anti-pimp message be heard?

"Our ancestors did not struggle for it to be like this," best-selling author Jill Nelson said to me one day with every bit of exasperation as you can imagine. "Forget turning over, Harriet, Malcolm; Martin—they are twirling in their graves, things are so awful. They are twirling and can't stop!"

Nelson is the patron saint of Black female journalists everywhere. Or maybe she's just mine. She rose to worship status when she wrote a memoir about the time she spent as a reporter for the *Washington Post*, and decided to call it *Volunteer Slavery: My Authentic Negro Experience*. As a Black journalist who has spent most of my career in mainstream media, I will forever be thankful for her words.

I was thankful again for the uncensored Queen of Speaking Up when, in one of the clearest signs of pimp praise, *Hustle & Flow*'s title song, "It Is Hard Out Here for a Pimp," by Three 6 Mafia, won an Academy Award in 2006 for best song. Upon receiving their Oscar, Three 6 Mafia had to be bleeped by network censors several times during their acceptance speech. Instantly, I could feel the ground rumble from all that twirling. And I knew I had to hear some of that Nelson-speak.

She didn't disappoint. In response to the Three 6 Mafia display, Nelson penned a column called simply, "It's Hard Out Here for a Sister. . . ." Not that I needed any reminding, but when I spoke to her about it, it was clear just how hard it is these days. In her impassioned rant that could itself have been bleeped by network censors several times, it was clear that she was Rosa Parks tired and sick of it all—the Pimp Oscar and so much more. For Nelson it wasn't just the obvious degradation of embracing a song whose melodic hook is "You know it's hard out here for a pimp / When he tryin' to get this money for the rent / For the Cadillacs and gas money spent / because a whole lot of bitches talkin' shit." It was the blatant celebration of mediocrity. (Ghetto!)

It means, Nelson argued, that, breaking with history's twice-as-good tradition, Black folks now could "get rich being just as mediocre and small-minded as the worst of white folks." And that was nothing to celebrate. She was tired of what was blasted on the radio assaulting her ears and of the videos on TV assaulting her eyes (both, presumably, assaulting her brain). She had had it with what she called the "hip-hop monster" that had made very few Black faces rich but many, many, many white faces richer. She feared that our soul that had been sold—at a discount—could never be recovered. And this angry Black woman was plain sick that, in her mind, people were *not* outraged by it all.

"Do we have a Black community worth preserving?" she demanded. "And what are we going to do to preserve it?"

I hate to admit it, but at the time I didn't answer.

Psssst, hey baby . . .

What are we teaching our kids about relationships? Chris, sixteen, from Brooklyn let roll off his tongue one day while sitting in my kitchen that he'd had sixteen exes. I had been talking with Chris, the type of kid you see around the way, about all things ghetto for most of the summer. At this confession, he was at the point where he was just starting to really open up, making our journeys together priceless. "All my buddies ask me about girls because I have sixteen exes," he said, his eyes as bright as the Jesus hanging from the platinum-esque chain around his neck. "They think I know a lot of things about girls." At the moment I couldn't shake the number. It sounded a bit ridiculous for a sophomore in high school. The chubby cheeks on his baby face couldn't even grow a whisker of peach fuzz, yet he claimed to already have been through a double-digit number of relationships.

Afterward it wasn't the number that stuck with me, though, it was the exes part. Chris didn't say he'd had sixteen girlfriends, but he thought of his relationships in terms of exes. It's a much more defeatist or negative way to look at these past couplings, especially for teenagers who are at the beginning of their romantic run and not in the jaded homestretch like my thirtysomething single girlfriends, divorcées, or anyone else who has been around and around the block. It is as if Chris never expected a relationship to last long enough to register more than being an ex.

Labeling these girls in his life as exes rather than former girlfriends helps to diminish their importance. These girls aren't even important enough to carry the girlfriend label at all. They are not ex-girlfriends but simply exes. The lingo has successfully depersonalized these relationships. There is no investment in an ex, it is just one of many. Just like in those videos there is never one dream girl but a harem of girls all ready and willing to get get get it poppin'.

Chris was able to rack up so many exes because his relationships generally didn't last longer than a few months. Appropriate for high school romances, I admit. His longest relationship lasted six and a half months, which is probably pretty good for a sixteen-year-old, and his shortest was three days. It ended when he found out that ex was in a gang, something Chris didn't want to have anything to do with. Appropriate and pretty good judgment for a sixteen-year-old. (He's not ghetto.)

Still, stuck on the no-hope of his ex lingo, I demand to know about the breakups. Why did most of these relationships end? It turns out that every one of Chris's exes, except the gang girl, cheated on him. Chris wouldn't talk about the first time it happened; it clearly still hurt. "I tried to cheat back a few times, but it felt worse," he said. Now he gives girlfriends one chance—one chance to cheat. Cheat once and there will be no breakup. But more than once and things are over. "I'm not going to be taken as a fool," he said.

Many folks dismiss teenage romances as insignificant, unimportant, not worth paying attention to. In some households dating is banned altogether; in others these puppy-love moments are embraced to the nth degree with boyfriends and girlfriends becoming almost extended parts of the family. Who knows which is better for long-term relationship health. But there is no denying that these first romances—

no matter how young (or old) the person is when they happen—are still the foundation to learn about what it means to be a couple. No matter how much parents want to believe these relationships are insignificant, they are often the first sexual experiences their children have, even if it is just a first kiss. These encounters thus help to shape our expectations of a mate and how we relate to potential suitors in the future. And even at these puppy-love stages we are already headed down the wrong track. Consider that a Gallup poll of thirteen- to seventeen-year-olds found that one in eight teens knows someone in an abusive relationship with a boyfriend or girlfriend.[9] One in eight! What are we teaching our kids about relationships?

Apparently, that infidelity, abuse, and overall disrespect are part of the norm. Ghetto.

Psssst, hey ma . .

When Bill Clinton's sex life became national news, what surprised me most, cigars aside, was the reaction, or rather nonreaction, of my mother. Forgive me for rehashing ancient news, but some events are too relevant to forget.

My mom, a lifelong Democrat, is a true party believer to the extreme and thus a major Clinton fan. Truthfully, "major" is probably an understatement. She stood on line for his book signings in Harlem for hours just to shake the man's hand. When she called me afterward I thought she was going to pass out from excitement. She fondly refers to him as "Bubba," as if he were in her inner circle. Her unabashed devotion to the man is a bit hard for me to fully comprehend, so I try not to bring it up because with her there is no rational conversation to be had on the subject. "Don't knock my Bubba." But strip away the politics, the overzealousness of a special prosecutor overstepping his bounds, bogus impeachment proceedings—at the end of the day Bill Clinton cheated on his wife. He is not the first man to do so and not the last.

He isn't even the first president (Thomas Jefferson, Grover Cleveland, FDR, JFK, and by some accounts in the grocery aisle, W himself). And he won't be the last.

Therefore it isn't his actions that I want to examine here. Instead, it is society's reaction to the news that I find most ghetto. Those who already disliked the president used the circumstances to feed their politics, masking it in discussions of character and dignity. Those who already liked the president used the circumstances to feed their politics, getting riled over the vast right-wing conspiracies and abuse of power. But, for the most part, the transgression did not change anyone's opinions of him; it just reinforced and impassioned feelings that were already there. There were even people who used the episode as proof that Clinton was a real man (whatever that means), one of us, even the first "Black" president. His weakness made him more likable in the eyes of some. In any case, the fact that the incident generally just strengthened existing opinions means that the act itself really didn't matter to any of us.

My mom doesn't even discuss Bubba's infidelity, dismissing the topic as if it were an annoying gnat buzzing around. My mom would probably be surprised to hear that I agree with much of her rhetoric—the politics of the episode—even though I fully admit that Bubba, the man, disgusts me. It wouldn't stop me from voting for the politician if I thought he was the best candidate, but I wouldn't want that man to be one of my husband's boyz.

This widespread shrug of the shoulders and nonreaction, like my mom's, over behavior that has always previously been considered the most shameful, I think represents a definite (ghetto) shift in what has become acceptable. It is a sign that our own relationships are in such shambles that instead of a shameful exception, Clinton stood as a reflection.

My good friend Jay, who can juggle relationships masterfully with his two wandering eyes, constantly argues that monogamy is not only a myth but unnatural. "I've cheated on every girlfriend I've ever had starting with my first back in high school," he told me. He put "cheated" in air quotes since he doesn't consider one-nighters with exes—something he'd done the night before, thus prompting our discussion—to be cheating. Jay, a thirty-three-year-old college-educated professional, goes to work every day to his good job. He comes from a close-knit, middle-class, two-parent family. And except for the whole (un)faithful thing, as far as I can tell, he's a very supportive boyfriend to any and all women he is involved with. At first glance most would not think Jay had so much in common with the knuckleheads on the corner. That's why first glances can be dangerous.

In a recent study of sexual behavior, University of Chicago researchers found that cheating is rampant. In one of the city's lower-income Black neighborhoods, for instance, one in five men was juggling two or more women at a time.[10] Before you get your ghetto-wagging fingers out, the same researchers found that two-timing was actually more common among better-educated African American men than among their lower-class counterparts. Because these "good men" are considered so rare, researchers concluded that women, so afraid of being alone, put up with such transgressions more and, at least unconsciously, almost expect them. Therefore, when it comes to relationships, my friend is not the only one whose mind is set on ghetto. "Monogamy," Jay reminds me one day, "is unnatural." Unnatural! After I stopped laughing at this player anthem, I thought about it. Could he be right?

A few years ago a book made a big splash by arguing scientifically that lifetime monogamy was indeed unnatural. *The Myth of Monogamy*, written by a zoologist and a psychiatrist, used DNA to study animals and found that species long considered to be monogamous, like geese, weren't actually so. They concluded that of the 4,000 mammals in the animal kingdom, only about 3 percent are actually monogamous, including bats and some foxes, and only 9 percent of the world's primates are monogamous. Based on their animal findings, with a heavy coating of psychobabble, the authors—a husband-and-wife team, in fact—then argued that monogamy was not natural, even for humans. Who knows if it is true or just the player anthem with numbers? I do think, though, that the fact that the authors managed to stay married through writing such a book is more stunning than what they actually wrote. (On second thought, maybe they both cheat!)

Certainly the white picket fence and "till death do us part" is not realistic for everyone. In fact, there are so many of us who fall into the "everyone" group that sometimes I think we should probably just end the thought at not realistic. My own parents were never actually married. Growing up I always felt their nonmarital status was my family secret. Now, looking at the state of families today, I guess my parents, for better or for worse, were ahead of their time. Still, I'm not ready to give up on the concept of commitment yet. And maybe that is something different from marriage, or rather, how most marriages are practiced. My non-married parents shared a home and a life for thirty years and were more committed to each other than many of us who have vowed to be committed.

But if Jay is right and staying faithful really is unnatural, then why hide, why creep at all? No matter what the on-the-side situation, the common thread is some level of secrecy. Why pretend that there is a commitment to protect? Because, the ideal of this lasting commitment (or what the fairy tales define as marriage) is still an ideal most of us think is worth striving for. "Despite the reality, every study shows that the vast majority of Blacks express a desire to marry," says Dr. Larry E. Davis, dean of the School of Social Work at the University of Pittsburgh.[11] (The reality is that while two-thirds of whites are married, about two-thirds of Blacks are single.) "A fulfilling, lasting relationship is still most people's goal." Davis should know. His book *Black and Single: Meeting and Choosing a Partner Who's Right for You* made the professor a best-selling author, not to mention a couch regular on the talk-show circuit and in women's magazines.

In fact, although the zoologist and the psychiatrist argued that monogamy might not be scientifically natural, they did not argue that it is unattainable. On the contrary, they insisted that "monogamy is the best path to a mature, deeper love."[12] In essence, monogamy is what advances humans beyond the animal kingdom. "The perfect fit of a good monogamous marriage is made, not born," they write. "And despite the fact that much of our biology seems to tug in the opposite direction, such marriages can in fact be made. It is an everyday miracle."[13]

Psssst, hey baby . . .

This overall support for marriage and commitment doesn't mean blindly pushing the white dress and chapel as the answer. About one-third of children born today are born to unmarried parents, compared to 6 percent in 1960.[14] Because the numbers tend to indicate that marriage is especially unpopular in lower-income households with children, marriage mistakenly often gets held up as the answer. As if the problems of these poor families would miraculously be solved once they walked down the aisle. To conventional, middle-class eyes and biases, what could be more ghetto than *not* marrying your babydaddy? (Or at least one of them.*) Fueled by church-funded studies, the second Bush administration has even proposed spending more than $300 million a year in welfare funds to promote marriage. The White House tends to focus on what it sees as the marriage magic window, the period right after an unmarried couple gives birth when dewy-eyed lovesickness is usually at a high point. There is some truth to the power of this

---

* Cheap, okay, very cheap, shot, I know. But how many of you were thinking the same thing? We be ghetto!

honeymoon period. The Fragile Families Study, an ongoing study of more than thirty-seven hundred low-income, unmarried couples in twenty U.S. cities, found that among such couples marriage talk was at a high point right after their baby came. Researchers found that 86 percent of unmarried mothers and 91 percent of unmarried fathers who were living together around the time their baby was born said they wanted to get married. Yet by the end of the year only 15 percent of the couples actually had.[15]

At first glance the president's Healthy Marriage Initiative can seem like a harmless appeal to bring parents to the altar. A quick fix to ghetto love. Even Dr. Davis, the relationship PhD, has argued in support of Bush's marriage initiative. But the danger in pushing marriage as the panacea is that you could be blindly advocating cementing relationships between people who sometimes have no business being joined for any period of time, let alone for life. There is no way I will be convinced that staying in a bad marriage is better for the children than trying to go it alone. What could be worse building blocks to give our children as they are learning to develop relationships than a household filled with abuse, disrespect, and animosity? That one-in-eight statistic on teenagers in abusive relationships is something we shouldn't forget.

Indeed, when the Fragile Families research is examined more closely, most of the couples in the study did not end up getting married primarily because of infidelity and drug abuse.[16] Those are very real issues that you'd hope would make anyone hesitate before jumping the broom. With that kind of dysfunction and instability, is getting married really going to help things? I doubt it.

Psssst, hey ma . . .

Part of what makes the blatant infidelity, babydaddies, on-the-side, Clinton, Jay, and the rest ghetto, and not just human nature or not, is the utter lack of shame that seems to accompany it. Usher is able to belt out confessions because he is not really confessing. Whether the antics are true or not, he is merely singing about a situation that has become not that big a deal in our ghetto world. Instead of not confessing, he's celebrating. Hence the bounce-your-head beat, cool dance moves, and the flash of abs. Can you imagine ex-cons singing in this way about the men they had raped in prison? Or child abusers about hitting their kids? Or pedophiles adding dance tracks to their molestation stories? (On second thought, R. Kelly's trash does hit number one. We be ghetto!) Call me crazy, but I just can't believe that if we were truly embarrassed about something the human ego would allow us to flaunt it. It is this wave-your-hands-in-the-air celebration—par-tay—about all these on-the-side situations, more so than the reality that they exist, that so desperately needs to go away.

Psssst, hey baby . . .

What we are really talking about (hoping for) is respect—of each other and for ourselves. That is what will wipe away these ghetto love stories. Or maybe it's the first step. Sounds too simplistic to be true, but respect really is at the root of healthy relationships. Understand that, and the luckiest of us will live happily ever after. The rest will be left with an understanding of commitment that allows us to flourish instead of being trapped in a cycle of devastation. Or, at the very least, demanding respect will eliminate the legitimacy of on-the-side.

Dr. Davis has been trying to teach this for a long time. Like a true social scientist, the psychologist has the respect thing boiled down to a formula. He calls it the Romantic Market Value, or RMV. Based on research he began in grad school, Davis applies an economic theory to the decision making of Black singles seeking relationships. Davis's formula to get that healthy relationship and respect is asking these questions: What realistically do you want? What realistically do you have to offer? and; What are you willing to do to adjust your RMV to fit someone else's RMV?

Respect.

Among my circle of close friends, I've been in the same committed relationship the longest. When I was the first of my crew to get married, everyone I knew was so far from that point in their minds and lives that the news—that someone they knew could be at that point—hit most of them like a shocking bolt of lightning. Our entire wedding party was single, so single that most didn't even bring a date to our wedding. Five years later, all were married to soul mates they had found since I jumped the broom. Through the years, being the hooked-up one amid a bunch of hard-core singles meant that I am always asked relationship advice. What's the secret?

Despite Davis's RMV index, there are no rules that are guaranteed to work. But after much thought I think the key to ward off ghetto love is to demand what you are worth . . . always. "When you love yourself, you know that you are valuable and you don't have to pretend to be anything but what you are," says relationship consultant Grace Cornish-Livingston, PhD.[17] Of course, it is much easier said (or written) than done. But the bar has to be raised, so I write.

Mr. Security Guard and I don't exchange hellos anymore. It turns out that turning down a hey-baby offer loud enough for the knucklehead's boyz to hear is a more surefire "end" in these ghetto times than flashing a wedding band and telling someone you're married.

Pssst, hey baby . . .

Tired of these hey-baby interruptions? Join the club. For women, interruptions like this are constant in our ghetto journeys. But since we are talking about relationships and the big "What does it say?" questions about mind-set and mood, it probably is a good time to dissect this constant interruption, as promised.

"Pssssst, Maaaaaaa, God bless your smile. You're beautiful, you know that? What's your name, baby? C'mon, you can tell me your name. I just want to be friends. You think we can be friends? Here's my number. You gonna call me? Please, baby, baby, please."

His voice is always low enough to make such intrusive banter private, even though it is usually delivered in the most public of spots—the street. Today he seemed young to me because he was so far from true manhood, propped up by his boys who crowded the corner and watched. It is a ghetto scene that plays out continuously in every city. Like a hunter in the woods, he doesn't really see me specifically, just fresh prey, which is endless. When he doesn't catch me, he will load up and shoot again at the next bird. To be fair, I don't see him, either, just another man-boy on the corner, and they are endless, too. Instead, from the instant the *psssst* passes his lips all I can do is wonder if there is a woman anywhere for whom this actually works. Like a child I cross my fingers and hope no.

Psssssssst, ma. The remarkable part about ghetto interactions is how deliberate they are. Which means that these conversations on the corner manage to masterfully say a lot to those who are willing to listen. Contrary to what most of us may like to think about behavior we wished would go away, everything is done for a reason. Ghetto, after all, is a choice. *Pssssssst, ma.* This universal catcall of every corner is the perfect opener. The affectionate generic nickname of the moment—mommi, boo, shorty, baby, ma, sweetheart—is especially good ammo for the shotgun approach when you try to hit (on) anything that walks by rather than someone whose name you might actually already know. After all, focused interaction like that takes work and could actually lead to a real relationship—of any kind. And if you're ghetto, by definition, significant relationships and work hold no appeal.

God bless your smile. I have values! I am righteous. I am not a bad guy—I believe in the Lord, damnit! So at what point do the continuous blessings—there are so many body parts, after all—heaped by the knuckleheads make them poster children for the Christian Coalition?

You're beautiful, you know that? I am going to force you to engage me by making you work for your compliment and ask you a question that you have to answer. Control is the goal, and because of low expectations the tiniest interaction like this is enough to satisfy the control fix. Don't worry, no matter what your answer, more chitchat will follow because with your answer, even a forced one, the toe is now in the door.

I just want to be friends. I am really a nice guy. There is nothing threatening about friendship.

Here's my number. The master player always offers his number instead of asking for yours, and, if anything, the knuckleheads know how to play. Offering his number makes him seem approachable with nothing to hide and gives the illusion that the decision is ultimately yours. Also, if anything goes wrong, it's your fault because you initiated the interaction by calling him.

Please, baby, baby, please. If it makes you feel better, blame it on Mars, either Blackman or the fourth planet where they say men are from. But, the truth is, anyone who has ever gotten a little somethin' somethin' ain't too proud to beg.

Tomorrow *he* will be different to the naked eye but everything else will be startlingly familiar.

Psssst, hey baby . . .

How We Roll

Driving a pimped-out ride with any or all of the following:

- rims that spin, that shine, that look more expensive than the car itself
- windows so tinted that some kind of military-grade night-vision goggles are needed to see out of them
- a TV and a video-game system
- a club-worthy sound system
- a custom paint job that includes images of flames in any capacity

. . . while still living at home with your mama

Leasing a car that you could never afford to buy

Driving a luxury car but still renting an apartment instead of owning a home

Driving a fortified Hummer as a civilian while soldiers at war drive unarmored Humvees

5

FAMILY VALUES

I see some ladies tonight who should be havin my baby, Bay-bee
—THE NOTORIOUS B.I.G.

True to my ghetto tastes, despite everything that New York City has to offer on a Friday night—the endless possibilities have drawn people from small towns everywhere—my favorite option is going to the movies. Actually I go on Wednesdays because it is easier to jump, so I get two flicks for the price of one. The going price for movie tickets in NYC is more than ten bucks, so jumping is the only way I can affordably feed my habit. On a rare occasion, I have jumped twice, sitting through three straight movies in their entirety. My only criteria for a jump-in is that I see the movie from the beginning—I cannot tolerate sitting down after the opening credits have already flashed. (I am not ghetto.) With those requirements I end up seeing a lot of bad movies, movies no one cares about, and I am often the only person in the audience on a Wednesday night, just because it was the flick that was next to start when my first movie was letting out. It was probably one of those Wednesdays in 2001 that got me watching *Hardball* with Keanu Reeves. In this stereotypical, against-all-odds, ghetto sports flick, Reeves plays a chronic gambler. To pay off his debts he ends up coaching a boys Little League team from the Cabrini—"Candyman, Candyman Candy . . ."—Green projects in Chicago. If you've ever seen *The Mighty Ducks, The Bad News Bears, Sunset Park,* or any other come-from-behind sports flick, then you've seen *Hardball,* although it does tend to be more entertaining than most.

In one of the mini-triumphs, one of the kids on the team can pitch (which not surprisingly he does magnificently) only while he wears his headset and listens to an endless loop of "Big Poppa." He even has a hand-wavin' move he always does on the mound on beat. As a result, throughout the movie the Biggie hook, "Cause I see some ladies to-night who should be havin my baby, / Bay-bee"* is uttered constantly. (By the time the movie hit the screens, the six-year-old aging rallying cry was already a bit stale, a sign that *Hardball* was definitely a product of "Hey, bro"-slappin' white men.) Nevertheless the hook was uttered constantly in the movie by everyone, from the struggling prepubescent Little Leaguers to the fans in the stands. In that one scene necessary for any Hollywood sports story involving a Black team—the one that shows that the little ghetto kids have finally gotten to their great white hope—Keanu Reeves even starts singing the hook in, of all places, an Irish bar. I think just for the comical imagery and ridiculousness of Keanu trying to rap, that scene had to be my favorite. And, yes, I'm laughing at him, not with him.

Sitting through *Hardball* reminded me how much I've always hated that song. Take away my Brooklyn creds, but Biggie's "Big

---

* To bounce your head to the full hook for "Big Poppa," check out one of the online lyric sites, like www.seeklyrics.com, which don't seem to worry about copyright infringement.

Poppa" goes down on my list of all-time least favorite songs. And it is because of that hook: " 'Cause I see some ladies tonight who should be havin my baby, / Bay-bee." The hook disturbs me even more than does the rapper's plea that "anyone with a gun up in their waist" not "shoot up the place." Because what Biggie is really doing is marking his prey. Like a male cat spraying its territory, he's spraying his conquests. That's why he says *ladies*, plural; if he were talking about just one woman, the hook could even be romantic. But with *ladies* all he's really talking about is building a stable of babymamas. I just can't throw my hands in the air like I don't care to that true player anthem, no matter how good the beat is.

Somewhere along the way having a baby has come down off its pedestal. It became no big deal, or at least not a big enough deal. How else could we all cheer during a kids' movie to "I see some ladies tonight who should be having my baby, / Bay-bee"?

Years ago I did once meet a woman, Dana, who had met her husband in a club. Her story still stands out in my mind because, despite what Biggie says, usually a club hookup is guaranteed not to lead to anything so significant. There are certain stories that married women, in order to illustrate their fairy-tale happiness, like to embellish and tell and retell when they are around other women. It is a form of passive-aggressive cattiness, a way for the I-have-a-man women to shout it to any woman caught listening and prove that her man is indeed worth having. For younger women, "The Proposal" tops the list, especially if the rocks that she got were significant. For the rest it is the moment— the meeting. Everyone has a story of how she met her husband. For romantics, it is a love-at-first-sight meeting. For realists it is a meeting. And for everyone it is going to be a memorable story, at least when it is told.

My story is embarrassing in its PG-ness. College party. Out on the lawn. A circle of people surrounded the pair, as is required whenever a couple is tearing up the dance floor. The stop-and-look groove from the circle was starting to tire, and the GO! GO! GO! chants from the crowd were quieting. I was outside the circle (very) quietly watching by the speakers. He was the one being cheered on dancing with some woman with equal skills. When it was all over and he ended up also standing on the side by the speakers to dot his sweating forehead and take a rest, I walked over and introduced myself. (Theme song: "I Wonder If I Take You Home," Lisa Lisa and Cult Jam.) He smiled. I smiled. All good. I took a chance and in a *Happy Days* moment invited him to pizza in that casual We're-all-going-to-get-pizza-now-wanna-come? kinda way. (It was college—game was not required.) He nodded. But when it was time to go, he did not budge. In a desperate attempt to act like we were all still on the same page, I nonchalantly said, "I guess I'll just see you over there." He nodded his head again. At the pizza place I helped my friends polish off a couple of pies while sitting next to an empty seat. My husband-to-be stood me up! The next time our paths crossed a few days later, caught up in that puppy crush, neither of us mentioned pizza, and things were all good again. It wasn't until after a month or so of constant weeks of hanging out, over pizza—a sign that we were indeed a happy new couple in that schoolkid way—that I found out that during that first smiling conversation by the speakers, he hadn't heard a single word I had said. This is usually when most women go "Awwww."

In all those stories I've heard—even the ghetto tale down in Jersey that started with "I met my ex-wife at Great Adventures," the amusement park in New Jersey that for the rest of the tristate area is known as Great Adventure—Dana was the only, *the only,* woman I had ever come across who had actually met her husband in a club. It's not that a man is never looking for a wife, but that when surrounded with alcohol, a booming system, and scantily clad bodies at their sexiest, it is a good bet that getting serious about anything is just not on the agenda. (*"12 a.m. on the way to the club / . . . 2 a.m. now I'm gettin' with her / . . . 5 a.m. now we at my house / 6 a.m. I be diggin' her out / 6:15 I'll be kickin her out / 7 a.m. Ima call my friends / 12 a.m. We gonna do it again"*—Jay-Z "Do It Again.") So when she told her story to the group of female strangers while watching her toddler run around the room at uncontrollable sugar-high speed. she almost whispered as if it was the most embarrassing moment she could tell. "Yeah, I met my husband at a club." Enough said. Unfortunately, it was. (She be ghetto.)

Riding on the subway I was not looking to find out how much our families are suffering, but discovered it anyway. The stranger sitting next to me during this journey was younger than me but didn't realize it. So he was a bit stunned when I turned down his hey-baby come-on by flashing my wedding ring. In an instant the conversation went from playful to serious.

"Married!" he gasped, his face visibly frozen in surprise. "I don't know if I could do that," he said, shaking his head as if he had just met someone who had climbed Mount Everest or parachuted from an airplane.

"You mean get married?" I had to check, because the marriage reaction is one of the first clues that I am slipping into ghetto territory. Not that that flash of commitment panic is reserved for the ghetto. Not by a long shot. But that the prospect of entering such a commitment seems completely inconceivable seems truly ghetto. Getting married is something that is so rarely done or seen as necessary that when I tell folks around my way that I am married, the response I regularly get is that look of sheer surprise. Even my own parents, who never married, were stunned when I announced my marriage plans. Their shock is forever captured on my wedding video. In other circles, however, the jumping of the broom is just so expected that people obsess over when, not if, it will happen. If it doesn't, it's a sign of failure.

"Yeah, married," he said. Then after a pause, he added: "I could have a baby but I don't think I could ever get married."

To me this was remarkable. Was he more scared of marriage than fatherhood? We talked for almost an hour on the long ride home from Manhattan to Brooklyn, each a mystery to the other. To him the permanency of marriage, the foreverness, made it scary. Understandable. But to me what could have more permanency and foreverness than raising a child? That was the biggest responsibility that anyone could have. In all truth, even with the best intentions, the strongest faith, the hardest of work, you may not stay married. But once you have a baby you will always be a parent. That is true foreverness.

"But once you have a baby, even if you don't get married, aren't you tied to your baby's mama forever?" I asked cluelessly.

"Nah, nah. That's different. That's different. I wouldn't be sharing my life with her, ya know what I'm sayin'," he answered cluelessly.

I didn't really. Neither of us was a parent at that point. Still, I couldn't understand how anything could be more of a commitment than having a child.

The misguidedness of a complete stranger with whom I talked for only an hour on the subway shouldn't have bothered me as much as it did, but I haven't been able to shake the conversation. I know his way of thinking is too common. I see the proof every day—those among us who just don't seem to understand the responsibility of parenthood. These are the people—whether they are A-list stars who leave their adopted babies in the care of others 24/7 day after day or young girls around the way hanging on the corner with their kids in their strollers at midnight—whose lives don't change once they have children.

What does that mean for families? Not the *Father Knows Best*, 2.5 kids, a dog, and garage families but real families. Families like mine, where mom and dad raised kids but never walked down the aisle. Single-parent families. Multigenerational households where grandma is raising the kids. Committed partners and same-sex partner families. As well as the married with 2.5 kids and a dog families. What does it mean for all of them? What does it mean if parenthood is taken for granted instead of worked at the way we take care of our bodies at the gym, or our wardrobes, or the stereo systems in our cars?

Again, it means we are breeding a generation of no hope.

Cornel West calls it nihilism. It is the devastating combination of "love-lessness" and "hopelessness." He speaks to "[t]he profound sense of psychological depression, personal worthlessness, and social despair widespread in Black America." The combination destroys a community from the worst possible place—from within. West argues that nihilism among Black people—"the lived experience of coping with a life of horrifying meaninglessness, hopelessness, and (most important) love-lessness"—is our "major enemy."[1]

I first heard West's thoughts on our self-destruction at a convention of Black journalists in Philadelphia. I was a young, new reporter and it was my first convention. I was still stuck at that local paper down in sub-urban New Jersey, drowning in small-town minutiae. I covered rural horse-farm country, which meant that the moment I set foot in town I doubled the Black population of the place. When I got to Philly, I was excited to shed my "only" status for a few days and be around some folks. West kicked off the convention with an early-morning session. By the end of his speech about lovelessness and hopelessness and the need for Black pride I was on my feet. (Toto, I wasn't in Jersey anymore!) That was more than twelve years ago. Unfortunately, West could have given the same speech yesterday. And that is what leaves me with a lit-tle hopelessness.

During the summer my journeys took me to a neighborhood arts festi-val in Brooklyn. On the soundstage was a day of young dance troupes. One troupe, young elementary school kids from the Red Hook projects, was hard to ignore. They called themselves America's Most Wanted even though none of their members could have been more than eleven years old. Seeing children excited about the art of dance—dabbling in choreography, working as a team, cultivating self-expression, interpreting music—was amazing. Seeing them use their talents and hard work to perform to "Back that ass* Up" (not the radio version of the song, either) was also amazing, in a scary, startling kind of way. The sexualized display of children grinding and seven-year-old boys mock-slapping the bouncing butts of seven-year-old girls was, well, you fill in the blank. And their parents proudly cheered their children on, the way every parent is supposed to cheer. Go AMW! Go! Go! Go!

It can be overwhelming—for all of us, since no one ever admits that maybe he or she is part of the problem. Shawn, thirty-six, in Chicago has come up with a unique solution. He is doing his best to climb to the top of the business world as if he's on a Black Power mission. So far, so good. After working on Wall Street for ten years, he started his own financial firm. The first in his family to graduate from college, he now flies first-class regularly to New York, mingles with bigwig money folk on Wall Street, and is the epitome of new Black elite success. Back in Chicago, he and his wife have four children. He gets lots of ribbing in his bourgie Black professional circles about the small tribe he's building at home. Most of his peers his age have just recently started their families, and their professional wives have no intentions of having even close to four children. But Shawn likes to joke that as an educated successful Black man he is just doing his best to counter the ghetto gene pool. "Tipping the scales" is what he calls it. "If all successful Black professional couples start having four, five, and six kids maybe we can tip the scales back, stack the next generation." I've never seen Shawn in an I ♥ BLACK PEOPLE T-shirt like the one that Mike in Chicago sported, but judging from their spilling "thoughts better kept secret," they are both rummaging in the same closet.

Shawn is hoping to counter families like Deke's in New Jersey. Deke also has four kids—but with four different women. Two of his daughters are only a few months apart in age, which means their mothers had to have been pregnant at the same time. It is something that is never mentioned by the women or anyone else. Deke's family was the first I had seen up close where there was always overwhelmingly many more kids than adults in the house. The youngest of ten kids himself and also his family's first college graduate, Deke owns his own home, which he shares with his ailing mother and his sister, who has her own three children by three different men. The result is constant chaos. Granted, Deke is more supportive—financially and emotionally—of his children than are most men in similar circumstances. But he's definitely the poster child for ghetto. The thing that really clinched it was the chaos. There is no order, reason, or dependability to his home life and by extension the lives of his children. As a result everyone ends up being responsible for himself, no matter how young. Simple routines like mealtimes or bedtimes don't happen. And rules don't seem to exist. Which means you can have a toddler with a bottle full of fruit punch sitting in front of a big-screen TV blaring the movie *Scarface*. When Pacino introduces his "little friend," the child watching jumped as each bullet is pumped. Or you can have a grade-schooler in desperate need of remedial help who comes home from school and can't find a clean, flat surface big enough to accommodate a sheet of notebook paper to do his homework, much less a quiet corner in which to think. Par-tay. And different women come in and out of Deke's house to drop off their kids at all hours as if this level of instability is acceptable.

My brain would argue that Shawn's holier-than-thou attitude about the ghetto gene pool puts him in the same company as Deke and his babymamas. Thinking that his bigger bank account is all he needs to keep his family from being ghetto is proof that Shawn's mind, busy tsk-tsking, does not understand what ghetto truly is. Still, I have to admit that my heart is rooting for more households that have the stability of Shawn's and not the chaos of Deke's. (I be ghetto.) I guess it is because chances are the future for Deke's kids is bleak compared to that of Shawn's kids. Nothing is guaranteed. Deke could be raising a future president and Shawn a career criminal. But it is easier to be trapped at the bottom than at the top.

In the 1960s Sen. Patrick Moynihan warned about this. Back then Moynihan was assistant labor secretary under Lyndon Johnson. After combing through pages of statistics, the young numbers cruncher came to a startling conclusion: the Black family was collapsing! Moynihan argued that families like Deke's are trapped in a "tangle of pathologies." High on his list of "pathologies" was babymamas. The stat man found that a quarter of all Black children were born to unmarried women and the percentage was rising. The tangle of poverty and despair was bleak, and Moynihan predicted it would get worse. Although the official name of the "Moynihan Report," as his research became known, was "The Negro Family: The Case for National Action," the only action that resulted was a reaction against the messenger's reputation. Criticism was quick and fierce. He was blasted by liberals for "blaming the victim," a catchphrase that was coined by his critics and entered the lexicon. Despite the widespread outrage, Moynihan's infamous "tangle" forever became synonymous with ghetto.

Now, more than forty years later, it is hard to miss that Moynihan got it partly right some of the time: things did get worse. But he also got it wrong: it wasn't just Black families that were headed for a fall but, as Ellis Cose argues, white ones, too. "Moynihan could not foresee that the statistics, so alarming about blacks, would eventually describe reality for many whites," says Cose.[2] Today one-fourth of all non-Hispanic white births are to single women. White women under age twenty-five are also more likely to have a child out of wedlock than in. Overall, one-third of American children are born to single women. This doesn't necessarily mean that these households are guaranteed to live in poverty and despair. But because of basic gender economics—women make (a lot) less than men in this country—the reality is it is more likely they will. And so these numbers basically imply that one-third of American children are more likely to be born into a "tangle of pathologies."

"It is like serving a sentence of twenty-five years."

"Twenty-five to life!"

They—Arlene and Pam—were talking about being a mother. The two older women telling-it-like-it-is were both newly retired. Their babies were all grown and starting to have their own babies. I had just met these women at their book club meeting, but that didn't stop me from bumming a free ride back to Brooklyn. Because I was the stranger in the group I was quickly forgotten in the backseat as the two old friends got into a rhythm, yapping about their years of hard work. They talked mostly about their kids and all the knuckleheaded things these grown babies were doing. One was going through a divorce. Another was moving back into his mama's basement. Another wasn't working up to his potential, stuck in a bad job too long. Blah blah blah.

The newest update was that Arlene had just gotten back from her first solo vacation since becoming a mother and had loved every minute of it. What made her cruise to the Caribbean truly a vacation, she said, was that it marked the first time in more than twenty-five years that she had focused on herself. She had not thought about her children for an entire week.

"It's like serving a sentence of twenty-five years" is how she described motherhood.

"Twenty-five to life!" Pam shot back.

Neither woman could have known that as I sat in the backseat I suspected that I might be pregnant. So when their tell-it-like-it-is hooting and hollering turned to the topic of children and family I couldn't stop listening to every detail. Admittedly, the sentence of twenty-five to life was a bit of a buzz kill for me in my initial pregnancy euphoria. But that's what our elders are supposed to do—pass on the truth and serve as a constant wake-up call. Aren't they?

It was also that moment that I realized that despite my every ungirly impulse and strong-willed independent woman ways, my whole life had been driven by the prospect of arriving at that moment I was finally at, right now, in the backseat of that car—becoming a mother. It was why I wanted a better life than what I had growing up, and why I had worked so hard to constantly do better. It was all for these supposed kids I hoped to raise one day. My success mattered so much because I wanted to create a world for them that was better than the world I had known. And that *is* a twenty-five-years-to-life job.

Unfortunately when the finger-pointing begins—about the lack of parenting skills, about not living up to responsibilities, and about the general breeding of knuckleheads—there is a tendency to wag those disapproving fingers at neighborhoods like my own of Bed-Stuy. That is the class snobbery that goes on, the assumption that parents in certain zip codes on the right side of the tracks are doing a better job than the others. It is the basis of Shawn's solution to ghetto. (And why it would never work.) According to that biased sliding scale, the farther down the income ladder you go, the worse parents you'll find. Logically we know class doesn't have anything to do with good parenting. Opportunities, yes. Money opens doors; grants opportunities, experiences, and access to a larger world. But it still does not guarantee better parents. While most of the kids growing up around my way became inner-city clichés—served time in jail, became parents too soon, landed in dead-end jobs—I ended up in a world far away from those streets, earning two Ivy League degrees and enjoying a successful career instead of a "job" like my parents. (I didn't even know there were so many people, besides models and Hollywood stars, with blond hair in this country until I went to college with all these rich kids.) Yet I did not get there because I was some kind of prodigy. I succeeded, in large part, because of my parents, and specifically because of their high expectations that kept forcing me to do better. At its simplest, class is not the only marker for parenting skills or lack thereof.

Instead, I think you can find examples in every social ranking, regardless of bank account size, of how parenthood has fallen off its pedestal. Unfortunately, ghetto mamas and papas are found on all rungs of the ladder.

In 2002 when thirty-six-year-old British-model-turned-actress Elizabeth Hurley gave birth to a baby boy, the man she said was her baby-daddy—mega-multimillionaire Steve Bing—in true ghetto fashion immediately denied he was the father. But a paternity test proved the real estate heir and sometime movie producer was indeed the dad. That same year Bing, whose net worth is estimated to be at least $400 million, was named in another Jerry Springer–like paternity claim. During child support proceedings between MGM Studios boss Kirk Kerkorian and his ex-wife Lisa Bonder, DNA tests revealed that Bing, not Kerkorian, was actually the father of Bonder's daughter. Ghetto. Despite Bing's obvious membership in the ghetto playa hall of fame, he went on to date Hollywood darling Nicole Kidman, who is often hailed for her motherhood dedication to two children she adopted with her ex Tom Cruise.

On our side of the pond, who could forget when after seven years, straitlaced Wonderbread actor Billy Crudup walked out on his girlfriend Mary-Louise Parker when she was seven months pregnant with their child so he could hook up with much younger, Yale-educated actress Claire Danes. Danes and Crudup are reportedly still together, and he's fighting Parker for visitation of their son; Parker won't allow her son to be in the same room as Danes.

I could devote an entire book to the ghetto ways of Britney Spears and her boy toy Kevin Federline. For the record, in case someone out there hasn't heard, to marry Britney, Federline also walked out on his longtime squeeze and babymama, actress Shar Jackson, while she was six months pregnant with their second child. (Although the former *Moesha* star is now permanently known as Federline's ex and the mother of two of his children, she actually has a total of four children—by two different daddies.)

But there are rich ghetto parents outside of Hollywood, too. Most recently the royal line of Monaco was thrown into clouded confusion when a French magazine ran a story claiming that in 2003 a flight attendant gave birth to the son of Prince Albert II, the heir to the throne. The woman lives with her son in a Paris flat owned by Prince Albert. Before the Royal Family could confirm or deny the rumor, photos surfaced of the prince with the African flight attendant, looking rather friendly. After assuming the throne the bachelor king admitted that the child was indeed his. Some worry that the king's love child would be the next in line to the throne. The woman claims not to care about her son's possible royal ascension. Instead she told the tabloid: "I wish simply that [Prince Albert] would assume some of his responsibilities."[3]

What's going on here is no different from the behavior most people think happens only in places like Bed-Stuy. The only difference is that when it happens around my way—fathers doing the kid's-not-mine dance or men leaving their pregnant girlfriends for their one on the side—folks are quick to say it is ghetto. And when it happens elsewhere folks say nothing at all. Yes, ghetto babymama drama comes in all wallet sizes.

In fact, using class as an excuse for bad parenting or no parenting is just a cop-out, a way to follow human nature and point your finger at someone else and tag them as lower. It is a way for us to avoid looking honestly at ourselves.

In reality, parenthood has become ordinary and is taken for granted, instead of worked at. That's why mothers are using their baby strollers as an accessory in their miniskirt maneuvers before sitting. That's why that guy I met on the subway ride home could be scared of the responsibility of marriage and not be scared of the responsibility of having a baby.

And that's why there are (too) many moments in the week when we'll see strangers on the street—children, mothers, families—and shake our heads because something just doesn't feel right with *those* people. The fact that we can continue to walk on by while shaking our heads shows, though, that something just isn't right with any of us. (We ghetto.)

I'm not an online junkie. I have no interest in chat rooms or message boards. I'm not a big IMer. I don't even know how to text message on my cell phone. But one day with too much time on my hands somehow I ended up on AOL's Black Voices portal. I have since become addicted to the Dirty Laundry question of the week. Reading through the subjects listed weekly on the message board is like eavesdropping. Guilty pleasure fun.

One day the dirty laundry question was about babymamas: "Is the term 'babymama' offensive? Is there a difference between a 'single mother' and a 'babymama'? Which term do you prefer and why?"

Sometimes questions are stop-in-your-tracks striking, particularly if you never realized there could be a debate on an issue. This was my reaction to "Is the term 'babymama' offensive?" How could it not be? I thought. Then again, I don't believe in calling myself 'nigger,' either, no matter what the spelling.

To me, there is something inherently condescending about the term *babymama*. "That's just my babymama." There was a one-hit wonder a few years back that captured the insignificance perfectly. "That's just my babydaddy" was basically the story of a woman convincing her new guy not to be jealous of some man buzzing around her. Why? "He's just my babydaddy," the chorus whined over and over again, and that alone was proof of the man's insignificance. The term *babymama* (or *-daddy)* implies that the couple is no longer together. Being a babymama is the only function she plays in his world. Otherwise he would say, there's my boo, girlfriend, wife, or even there's Cora. (Sometimes using someone's actual name can be the most intimate label in a world of multiple interchangeable partners.) Think of how different it is to say "That's my babymama" or "There's the mother of my children," or even "There's Jane's or John's mom." Instead, *babymama* is dismissive, loaded with disrespect for the woman and disrespect for the importance of the job of motherhood.

Interesting how every single person who replied to the message board to say without a doubt it was a negative term was male. One guy wrote that the women he calls his babymamas were nothing more than "receptacles," hence the nickname. And, sadly, the people who wrote in to defend the term were mostly women. At least when the knuckleheads call each other Nigger they are under the delusion that they are turning a negative into a positive. (Nigga, please! And the tooth fairy is real, too.) But here with the babymama defense we have an instance of the expectations of these women having gotten so low—meaning that they would never expect to have a lasting supportive relationship with the father of their children—that they don't even realize when they are being disrespected anymore. The American Idol and babymama Fantasia even made "Baby Mama" a hit single. Her B-A-B-Y M-A-M-A anthem applauded single motherhood, she told anyone who would listen. Women like Fantasia don't understand that *babymama* is disrespectful because they have been infected by ghettoitis, a devastating illness in which ghetto infects the mind so thoroughly that thinking logically is impossible. Disrespect is disrespect, even if you don't S-A-Y S-O. Unfortunately, ghettoitis is also highly contagious.

Of all the movies I see, my favorite type is horror films. I've seen hundreds. And on the rare occasion when a horror film is good, I'll scream and jump right on cue no matter how many times I've seen it before. Only recently have I come to admit that some of the most horrific stories imaginable can be found in the newspaper. That is how I felt about a year ago when I came across this story about the horrors going on in a neighborhood in Queens. This is how the story began:

On Christmas night at the Ocean Village apartments in the Rockaways, teenagers were setting fire to the holiday decorations in the hallways.

This was not remarkable in itself, residents said—hallway fires were routine, and teenagers had been burning wreaths and bows off apartment doors all week.[4]

I had to read these two sentences a few times before I could even believe what I was seeing. But the story gets worse. A security guard patrolling the building decided he would try to do something about the fires. When the guard, Raymond James, thirty-two, came across a smoldering shopping cart in the hallway of the fifth floor, he dragged it into the elevator to take it outside. After the doors of the elevator shut, the cart burst into flames. By the time the elevator got to the lobby, James, a father of four, had burned to death. Two thirteen-year-olds were charged with the murder. With the paper on my lap I sat in my kitchen and screamed.

Then the paper the next day ran a follow-up story with the headline MOTHER DEFENDS SON, 13, IN PRANK TURNED FATAL FIRE.[5] This is where things get undeniably ghetto.

Sitting outside family court in Queens awaiting the hearing for her son, Adalia Johnson, thirty-three, started passing the blame. The police had charged the boys with second-degree murder, but city prosecutors, concerned with their young age, had not yet signed off on the charges.

Inside court, after a half-hour hearing, Judge Edwina Richardson-Thomas ordered the boys to be held in police custody. "I do find these children would be likely to commit other acts of delinquency," she said, also ordering news organizations not to print the boys' names or identifying details.

This did not stop Adalia from talking to the media about her son as soon as the hearing was over. According to the mother, the thirteen-year-old cousins were "typical teenagers," students at the local junior high school, and devoted to sports and church. According to neighbors, many of whom admitted living in constant fear in their own building, the boys were fond of breaking glass and starting fires.

"The charges are overbearing," Adalia Johnson said about what her son was facing. "I feel sorry for the man, I feel sorry for his family, but I feel sorry for myself."[6]

As the fire department hailed the security guard as a hero for his actions, which, they said, prevented further harm and damage, the boy's mother went on to blame the guard for his demise, arguing that his actions "lacked common sense" because people are taught to flee from fires. In other words, it was Raymond James's fault that he burned to death Christmas night because he was stupid enough to try to do something about the mayhem her son and his cousin created in the building they called home.

I couldn't believe this "mother." There is a difference between coming to your child's defense and making excuses. No mother wants to see her child sent off to jail, but sometimes being a mother is having to admit that your child has done something wrong.

In fact, one of the biggest complaints of teachers these days is not about students but about parents.[7] That's because whenever they have to tell parents that their children have done wrong, the parents routinely argue.

"Not my child."

It is the teacher who is mistaken.

It is the school that is being too harsh.

"My kids aren't that bad."

Veteran teachers argue that they are seeing in children as young as six or seven a level of disdain for adults that once was seen only in teenagers. Parents have even sued schools that expelled kids for cheating, on the grounds that teachers had left the exams out on a desk and made them too easy to steal.

"They'll misbehave in front of you," complains Marcia Jones, a second-grade teacher in Murfreesboro, Tennessee. "You see very little of that 'I don't want to get in trouble' attitude because they know Mom or Dad will come to their defense. You get savvier children who know how to get out of things. Their parents actually teach them to lie to dodge their responsibilities."[8]

"I called the parents on a discipline issue with their daughter," says Greg Sarette, a grade-school music teacher in Lakewood, Colorado. "Her father called me a total jerk. Then he said, 'Well, do you want to meet someplace and take care of this man to man?'"[9]

Sitting in the park around my way one afternoon, I was nosily watching three mothers gabbing as their young children played. A young mother came marching over to the group. "Is your son in the orange?" she asked to no one in particular. It took a moment for any of the three to fess up to being the one to dress her son in prison colors. Until that moment, the mother of Orange Boy was actually the quietest of the three. "He broke my son's gun," the indignant mother accused, flashing a broken black toy gun that looked disturbingly real. All three women just stared back at her with "so what" blankness. I squirmed on my bench for a better view just in case a fight erupted between the mamas. (My ghetto side made me do it.) "He broke my son's gun. He broke my son's gun. It's broke. It's broke." Finally the mother of the orange-clad gun breaker responded: "What do you expect? He's only four years old." She then turned back to her friends to talk. That was it. She didn't call her son over, didn't get off her bench to ask her son if he had indeed broken another child's toy on purpose, and if so, dispense the minimum of a "don't do that" warning. Instead she just sat there while her two friends rolled their eyes at the nerve of the young mother, talking loud enough for all us nosey folk to hear, saying "How expensive could that gun be anyway?" To make the point, one of the women then reached into her tight jeans pocket, took a dollar out, and mockingly threw it at the mother holding the broken gun. The young mother raised the gun, which, again, looked disturbingly too real, paused, and bent down and scooped up the dollar from the ground before marching off.

Likewise, in the Ocean Village, Queens, case, the mother quickly dismissed accusations by her neighbors that her "churchgoing, sports-loving" boys were terrorizing the building by saying that it couldn't be true because they had never had run-ins with the law. "If they were bad kids, they would have been in the system before," she said. My kid is an angel because he's never been arrested? Run-ins with the law are now the standard we use for judging good behavior?

This distraught mother was not the only one making excuses. The neighborhood was making excuses, too. It reminded me of my disastrous subway ride when Red-T and his buddy the Screamer waved a gun for fun in their fake stickup. When the two were hauled off by the police, some passengers in the subway car tried to argue with the cops, as opposed to being appalled by the children's behavior.

Admittedly, life in the Ocean Village apartments puts a new spin on bad. The building is one of a series of drab, beige boxes—stunning examples of nondescript seventies architecture—that sit along three blocks of ignored oceanfront. The beachfront, instead of making the complex desirable, serves to isolate it from the rest of the city, limiting access to public transportation. Residents there live in fear of one another. As they speak in hushed tones and avert eye contact, they explain how avoiding putting Christmas decorations (or even doormats) outside their door is necessary for survival. At the least, the items would go missing and at the worst, they would be set on fire.

"You come back home and your doorbell's burned," said a forty-six-year-old woman, afraid to give her name for fear of retaliation. She has lived this way in this building with her husband and two children for fourteen years.

"The kids are wild, they're bad," said Jason, twenty-five, who lives nearby and visits Ocean Village often. Referring to a group of children who roam the neighborhood, he said, "They're thirteen, but the way they think, they're not thirteen."

Crime there is so rampant that one police officer described the building as "out of control."

I found no one who seemed surprised that the recklessness of two thirteen-year-olds ended up killing someone. Instead, residents pointed fingers. The real problem, they argued, was that the community center had closed a few years before. Now, residents complained, the kids had nothing to do. I was tempted to suggest "homework" but held back because does it matter? A man is still dead. Raymond James left behind a wife and four children, including a nine-month-old daughter named Antoinette. Whenever she sits on her mom's lap she shakes her rattle and utters, "Da-Da, Da-Da."[10]

The Ocean Village story is not just a tragedy; it's a ghetto tragedy. On one side four children are left without a father, and on the other side two boys are headed to jail before puberty. Adalia Johnson says her son and nephew are "sad and scared." Well, Ms. Johnson, I am, too.

. . .

I love it when you call me Big Pop-pa . . .

So Biggie's hook haunts me. Yes, it is all about the ladies/babies shout out. I find nothing endearing about those words being the rallying cry for twelve-year-old Hollywood Little Leaguers. This is not macho fantasy anymore, but the reality of our ghetto life.

And I'm tired of seeing some babies tonight who should not be havin' babies, Bay-bee.

6
NIGGA WHAT, NIGGA WHO

"What up, nigga."

"What up, dawg."

"You see that shorty last night? She looked nice. Not the big girl, the one wit the cellie blowin' up."

"Yeah, she looked tight. I think she gotta man, son."

"She had no ring. He not around, not my problem. You leave your drink around me, believe your drink gonna get drunk up.* Leave your girl, nigga, she gonna get took up."

"I'm just sayin'."

"Good lookin' out. Like I said to that bitch last night, 'Is ya man on the flo? If he ain't, let me know. Let me see if you can run it, run it girl.'"†

"Awwwww, shit. You hit that?"

"No doubt, no doubt. She know the game. I keep it real, straight-up. Raw, baby."

---

* "Stay Fly," by Three 6 Mafia.
† "Run It!" by Chris Brown featuring Juelz Santana.

"Holla! But be careful, son. Now I ain't sayin' she a gold digger, but she ain't messin' wit no broke niggaz.* Eighteen babies bring the karats. Straight-up."

"I don't even gotta worry 'bout that shit. Bitch like that—who knows where she been. No way she can pin some shit like that on me. Never know if that kid be mine. If I'm not a hundred and ten percent sure then it not my problem."

"I'm just sayin', son."

"Hey girrrl."

"Hey girrrrl. You look good. What happened with that nigga last night?"

"Don't know yet. Betta be street if he lookin' at me."†

"Take a chance, you stupid ho."‡

"My phone's ringin'. It's him. Trifling. Why is his ass callin' me already? I drive these brothers crazy. I do it on the daily."§

"You gotta handle your business. Anyway, what's goin' on with your boo? Girl, I can tell he's been lyin' and pretendin' that he's faithful and he loves you."||

"That my heart, you know that."

"You should call that nigga back from last night and make yo man jealous. Give him back some of what he be givin' you. Do them boys like they used to do you."**

"You right. You right."

▪ ▪ ▪

---

* "Gold Digger," by Kanye West featuring Jamie Foxx.
† "Soldier," by Destiny's Child.
‡ "What You Waiting For?" by Gwen Stefani.
§ "My Humps," by Black Eyed Peas.
|| "Girl," by Destiny's Child.
** "Independent Women, Part 2," by Destiny's Child.

"Much respect. Much respect. I hear what you be sayin'. I got kids already. I ain't tryin' to have any more jus' yet. They mamas always be tryin' to drag my ass to court. But Ima good fatha to my kids. No worries."

"No doubt. Let's get ignant, let's get hectic.* Aiiiiiiight. That's what I say."

"Yo, my phone, son. Here she is now."

"Who this?"

"Hey, baby."

"Hey, ma."

"My girls wanna go back to the club tonight. What you think?"

"What you got on, sexy?"

"Nuttin'. I'm just sittin' here waitin' for you."

"Don't go out with your girls, ma. I got you. I'll take you to the candy shop. I'll let you lick the lollypop."†

"You nasty. You comin' over tonight?"

"Let me call you back, ma."

"For real? Don't have me be waitin' for you all night."

"My dawg is hollin' at me. I'll call you back, ma. Peace."

"What he say, girl?"

"Oooooh girl. I did it again. Played with they heart, got lost in the game."‡

"It's time to get yours. As much as that other fool accused you of cheatin', you might as well had. Better get you some."§

■ ■ ■

---

* "Let's Get It Started," by Black Eyed Peas.
† "Candy Shop," by 50 Cent.
‡ "Oops . . . I Did It Again," by Britney Spears.
§ Inspired by "I Should Have Cheated," by Keyshia Cole.

"Yo, son, I ain't gonna front. Bitch blew my mind last night, dawg. She a freak. She gettin' crunk in the club. You know how I like to see the female twerking. Taking the clothes off buckey naked. Know what I mean?"*

"Fuck the club, dawg, I rather count a million bucks.† Gotta get rich—"

"Or die tryin'."

"Road trip, yo—I'm traffickin' in the white. America got a thing for this gangsta shit. They love me."‡

"I got you, son. Hustling, baby. Be the weatherman, make that snow. Dawg."

"I'm broke as a mofo, dawg."

"That why you don't need to be messin' with that shorty from last night. Focus. Focus. I hear her man is no joke, straight-up. That nigga keep it gully all the time."

"Niggas just runnin' they mouth. I come from Bed-Stuy, niggas either do or they gon' die. Brooklyn don' run, we run shit."§

"Believe that."

"Peace."

---

* "Get Low," by Lil' Jon and the East Side Boyz.
† "Soul Survivor," by Young Jeezy featuring Akon.
‡ "Hustler's Ambition," by 50 Cent.
§ "Lighters Up," by Lil' Kim.

7

SCHOOL ME

WATUP, watup, watup? The quickness of the familiar greeting made it impossible to hear when one word ended and the next began. Instead it was all one long utterance, punctuated with fist and chest pounds around the circle. The group of teenage young men in long—longer than that, longer than even that—white T-shirts (Tall Ts), baggy jeans, do-rags, and sneakers, were standing outside Boys and Girls High School in Brooklyn. This time the greeting was followed with "Didya-pass?" It was the last day of school and students were picking up their report cards. I was up in the mix as the ghetto explorer. My journeys around the way were so frequent these days that folks no longer asked me what I was doing with my notebook in hand. It was obvious: how we are livin' needs to be documented. "Didyapass?" was uttered so many times that afternoon that I wished it were some new slang that my adult ears didn't understand. It wasn't. The marker for success that day outside this typical urban high school was whether or not you would have to go to summer school. No summer school automatically meant you had done well. The specifics didn't matter. Those who escaped the summer school fate visibly rejoiced with hugs and laughter. Those who weren't so lucky were laughed at (this was high school, after all) and hugged. "Yeah, I got summer school this year," said one fourteen-year-old girl named Binka, according to her birth certificate and the old-school silver name-plate belt around her hips. She was standing off to the side alone to spare herself from her friends' constant taunting. "Hey B, what you do-ing this summer again?" "B, you gonna take the short bus to class this summer?" "Binka, you go to summer school so much they need to be calling it Binkaschool."

Because for so many the "didyapass?" moment was such a close call, that day quite a few mothers insisted on marching their teenagers to school in order to hear the summer school news themselves. After-ward, the yelling, the stern looks, the cold-shoulder disgust of these mothers when they marched their teenagers out of the building was a sign that the news wasn't good.

"I told you," one mother said to her son in her best sick-and-tired tone. "I told you. Even with summer school you are still going to have to be a freshman again in September. Your friends," she hissed with mocking sarcasm, "can't help you now."

As this mother shook her head and slapped her knee, instantly I got the "I'm sorry" chills as if I were a teenager myself. Her son, in perfectly matching mustard yellow polo and do-rag, Timberlands and cap, seemed to be immune to his mother's scolding, though not missing a single opportunity to offer a "watup" to the endless supply of his boyz passing by, during his mom's lecture as the two walked down the street.

The dangers of low expectations are most vivid and devastating when it comes to education. "I gotta graduate from high school so I can prove everybody wrong," said Chris, the sixteen-year-old with all the exes. He should have been going to summer school but instead would be repeating his sophomore year. "Everyone thinks I'm gonna drop out, my grandmother and ma tell me all the time."

It is important also to note that these aren't just the expectations that are placed on us by those we keep close in our world; they are also the expectations of those who should not matter from the outside world, as well as the expectations we hold for ourselves. In the case of the mustard-yellow-clad failure of a student being chewed out by his mother outside of Boys and Girls on the last day of school, his mother's head-shaking presence is a sign that she expected more from her son. Still the boy didn't seem to care that he had failed the ninth grade, so obviously he is fulfilling low expectations coming from somewhere.

From the outside, Boys and Girls High is beautiful. It's an enormous, fairly modern (by NYC public school standards) building of sleek red brick that stretches two entire square blocks and holds about four thousand students. If it weren't in Bed-Stuy, the school, with its stunning athletic fields, looks like it could be a suburban realtor's dream. Instead, one of the first signs that you are approaching the urban campus is a mini police substation that sits at the corner of Malcolm X Boulevard on the school's east border. The structure is permanently welded to the concrete, which means that the NYPD is guaranteed to leave a lasting impression at Boys and Girls even if the students may not.

On the inside, Boys and Girls is, simply, not a great school. It is an unremarkable neighborhood public high school in one of the city's neediest neighborhoods. The graduation rate is about 66 percent. Could be worse (the city's average graduation rate is between only 43 percent and 53 percent),[1] but it could be a lot better. This is the school that Aisha's parents, hoping she will be successful, refuse to send her to. Boys and Girls, like most of the nation's public schools, rides the middle of mediocrity. In fact, the school is so typically average in all its failure, shortcomings, and general badness, it is the Joe school of boys and girls everywhere.

When I went to high school in Brooklyn, I had no idea where Boys and Girls High physically stood; I just knew that it was the "rough school" whose students beat up the students at my "academic" high school, Brooklyn Tech. Tech was one of the city's three specialized high schools that required an entrance exam, attracting applicants from across the city. If the kids at Boys and Girls were the thugs, we were the geeks.

Those myths shattered during my sophomore year. One day we were let out of school early because the word *Decepticons* had been mysteriously spray-painted outside on the sidewalk. It was, indeed, the clichéd New York City hood moment. (Theme song: "Rockit" Herbie Hancock.*) As if on cue my entire class crowded by the windows to catch a peek at the big, bright tag below. Even from the sixth floor, standing several bodies deep, we could see every spray-painted stroke clearly. If the handiwork seemed too colorful to be menacing, the boldness of the move made up for it. The Decepticons, which took their name from the old Transformers cartoon about a band of robots that could transform from trucks and cars to missile-shooting figures, were a local gang from another time. Fearing that some kind of *West Side Story* brawl was sure to break out, school officials in full alert filed us out of the building. The rumor for a hot moment was that those responsible for the gang signature were from Boys and Girls.

It wasn't true.

In reality, New York's Decepticons gang had actually been founded by a group of former honor students at my own supposedly "far from rough" high school. (Ghetto.) In fact, the story gets even more ghetto: the Decepticons' coming-out party happened, of all places, during a March of Dimes walkathon circa 1985.

March of Dimes invented the walkathon, and the annual event is the primary fund-raiser for the charity, attracting thousands of folks eager to do good. The entire day Manhattan's Fifth Avenue is covered with shoulder-to-shoulder people extending farther than the eye can

---

* Leave it to a jazzman to create one of the best break-dancing beats of the decade and turn anyone with a pulse into a B-boy. Follow that leader.

see. From Central Park to the southern tip of Manhattan the mass walks waving signs, walks singing songs, and walks tired. It is the type of long, exhausting day that bonds people—for good and bad. Every year at Tech there was a huge drive by the gym teachers for volunteers for the walkathon. As a result, at some point, it ended up being something most of the school's "good students" did, gang-members-in-training included.

"The walkathon was hell to pay on some people. It was crazy that day, and we were wilding, we were out of control," remembers Shockwave, a former Decepticons member who was a sophomore at Brooklyn Tech the day of the walkathon. "Our earliest jump-off was just snatching chains—the knockout or snatching chains. So that walkathon was crazy."[2]

And so a gang is born. A group of smart friends from an elite school started snatching chains while participating in the ultimate goody-goody fund-raiser event. (Ghetto.)

The Decepticons were a real thug fest, though, and soon moved from fund-raisers to subways, where their specialty was robbing and terrorizing folks during runs between Brooklyn and Manhattan. The most interesting thing about the Decepticons was that despite all the hype they got, which was a lot in the eighties, the gang was mainly active during the school week, according to the gang unit records of the NYPD. On weekends, incidents involving Decepticons members barely surfaced.[3] I'd bet that the weekend falloff was probably a result of the double life these "good" kids were living.

Regardless of the truth, that afternoon as we were ushered out of school under a cloud of fear, the immediate impulse was to point fingers at Boys and Girls. After all, in many of our minds, those kids were the furthest thing from ourselves. But then that is how the ghetto blame game goes, doesn't it?

I still haven't gotten used to the fact that I now live a few blocks away from the infamous Boys and Girls High of my youth. On an oppressively muggy day at the end of the school year, I sat in Fulton Park and watched the teenagers I always assumed were so rough leave school. Now, to my adult eyes, they all looked, well, young. It was a sea of guys in clothes that could not get any bigger and girls in clothes that could not get any smaller. And all of them looked like they were going anywhere but school. High school, with its span of fourteen- to eighteen-year-olds, has always been a jarring mix of boys and men, girls and women, at least on the outside.

That day after school, boys hoping to be men strutted out the doors with pimp-walk perfection, the mandatory scowls across their faces, trying to ooze don't-mess-with-me menace. I tried to count how many male students I saw actually smiling, but the smiles were so few and far between I kept forgetting my count. Girls thinking they were women turned heads as they strutted with complete confidence, dripping sexuality to spare at a level that was once reserved only for the bombshells of the 1950s. The message blazoned across the bulging chest of one woman-child clad in a tight pink and white mini tank top read TOO SEXY. How true it all was. Only the faces of all these grown bodies betrayed how young these boys and girls really were.

The worst thing about this Joe school hits you right when you walk in. Over the school's front door is a dirty old banner that touts that Boys and Girls High is the "pride and joy of Bed-Stuy." Thinking back to the school's 66 percent graduation rate, the banner is almost mocking in its pep-squad cheerleading.

When it comes to education, the schooling of our children, there is a general consensus that something isn't working. It's something worse than a money-deprived school system, overcrowded classrooms, and declining test scores; it's something in the mood—if you try to pinpoint anything more specific, that's when everything gets fuzzy. But that feeling is still there deep in our gut, that things *have* changed—from our attitudes about education to its importance in our lives. That is why, for instance, Barak Obama could get a standing ovation during the Democratic National Convention when he called on parents to turn off the TV! It is also why during a Tyler Perry play a tangential scene in which the title character, Madea, takes a belt to a teenager who refuses to do her homework can get an Amen applause so stirring that the show is forced to come to a momentary halt.* And why a Joe school like Boys and Girls, with its "didyapass?" and 66 percent graduation rate, can be so upsetting.

But the hard-core facts—like the Decepticons ties to Tech—don't always coincide with what we think is true. The business journalist in me likes numbers. If there is a trend, then there has got to be some numeric statistic out there supporting it. Although there is not much formal research tracking attitudes toward education, most of what's out there tends to support the exact opposite of what our finger wagging insists is true. When asked, parents say they still find their children's education more important, not less, and the importance of education tends to rank highest among parents of color.[4]

This does not mean that (numerical) proof of our low expectations can't be found. For instance, in Michigan a recent study stunned educators when it revealed that school just was not that important to many parents in the state. Nearly half of the Michigan parents surveyed responded that they would not mind if their kids didn't end up going to college. Only 27 percent said that getting a good education is essential for getting ahead in life And three out of five parents defined success for their children without reference to education or the ability to support themselves.[5]

Newspaper editorials started calling Michigan—with one of the lower percentages of college graduates and one of the highest jobless rates in the nation—the new Mississippi. Surprisingly, residents didn't complain about the media's finger-wagging characterizations but in-

---

* I took in the Tyler Perry show at my local chitlin-circuit playhouse to check out the ghetto crowd who consider that hot ghetto mess to be theater. Yes, I said it! And I be ghetto.

stead defended their low expectations, criticizing the media, the governor, and educators for classism and snobbery.

The Michigan study helped soothe my journalist bones for the moment. (And made me for a finger-wagging instant happy that I don't live in Michigan.) But it was the other studies that bothered me a little more. I don't believe our guts are wrong. Things have changed.

A few years ago controversial anthropologist John Ogbu, who coined the term "acting white" to explain why some Black students seemed to shun doing well in school, unveiled an even more explosive study about Black middle-class students in the bourgie community of Shaker Heights outside Cleveland. In pointing the finger back at parents instead of at "the system," the late scholar (he died a few months after his book on the study was published) drew criticism, often angered and impassioned, from both his colleagues and the community.

Looking back, it becomes harder to ignore what Ogbu was trying to say.

Ogbu was invited to Shaker Heights not by school district administrators or teachers but by Black parents themselves. They wanted to know why their children—the sons and daughters of doctors, lawyers, judges, business execs—were doing so much worse in school than their white classmates. Although Black students in the middle-class district were some of the best students in the state, they were still lagging behind whites in the district in terms of grade point average, standardized test scores, and enrollment in advanced-placement courses.

Unfortunately, the situation sounded like my own high school experience. While my good school was approximately 60 percent Black, I would typically find myself among the same small bunch of Black students in all of my AP and honors classes. By the time I was a senior, when my schedule was filled with nothing but demanding classes, I had virtually no Black classmates, even though I was attending a Black school. Truth is this gap between white and Black achievement, as it has come to be known in the talk-show circuit, was popping up in schools across the country. The gap is what partially inspired Bush's controversial No Child Left Behind Act. The federal law requires schools to publicly report their performance data for the first time by race and ethnicity. Schools that do not produce acceptable test scores for all students are punished with a variety of economic sanctions. (Of course, this is a backhanded way to put the cost of the problem on local taxpayers, who end up paying more while the Feds get off the hook. Ca-ching.) Still, judging from the federal legislation, the Shaker Heights phenomenon was more common and widespread than any of us would like to admit.

After much coaxing, the parents convinced Ogbu, an anthropology professor at UC Berkeley who had spent his career studying academic achievement among different ethnic groups, to come to Ohio and study Shaker Heights. The school district agreed to finance the professor's research, and so Ogbu moved to Ohio for nine months. The result was the 2003 book *Black American Students in an Affluent Suburb: A Study of Academic Disengagement.* *

Ogbu concluded that Black students in Shaker Heights weren't doing as well as their white counterparts because their parents didn't stress education enough. It was disengagement of the worst kind. Ogbu acknowledged that other factors had a definite effect on academic achievement. The primary culprits were low teacher expectations (one teacher routinely chastised white students for coming to class late but not Black students, even when they came later—I guess CP time from *those* people is just universally expected now), prejudiced personnel, and other baggage associated with race. Still, with all that, Ogbu also faulted the efforts of the Black students and their parents. Despite parents' obvious concern, illustrated by the fact that they invited the anthropologist to come and have a look to begin with, Ogbu concluded that many of the same Black parents did not stress homework, attend

---

* *Disengagement* is academic speak for "don't give a fuck," as the corners would say.

teacher conferences, or push their children to enroll in the most challenging classes *as much* as their white counterparts did. In addition, he suggested that the Black students suffered what he termed "low-effort syndrome," meaning they didn't work as hard even though they knew how much work was needed to succeed in the Shaker Heights schools. Blame it on the low expectations of parents, teachers, and students; discrimination; and lack of role models—Ogbu argued all of the above. The bottom line is that whatever the causes, Black students were not working up to their potential.

"What amazed me is that these kids who come from homes of doctors and lawyers are not thinking like their parents; they don't know how their parents made it," Ogbu said at the time. "They are looking at rappers in ghettos as their role models; they are looking at entertainers. The parents work two jobs, three jobs, to give their children everything, but they are not guiding their children."[6]

Before Ogbu's book even hit the stores the criticisms started. The parents who had begged him for answers turned their backs when they did not like the answers he offered. One Black parent from Shaker Heights told CNN that the professor was an "academic Clarence Thomas." Others merely argued that his conclusions were outrageous, wrong, and misguided; they even suggested that the Nigerian immigrant did not fully understand the Black experience in America. Academics blasted his research methods. And, finally, the National Urban League sent out an official press release to condemn him and his work, stating: "The League holds that it is useless to waste time and energy with those who blame the victims of racism."[7]

Indeed, anything that even hints at blaming the victim is dangerous. It lets any other contributing factor (in the case of the Shaker Heights schools, racism) off the hook. The easiest thing to do once the victim is in any way blamed is to sit back and point the finger and refuse to listen to anything else, thereby allowing any other legitimate contributing factors to be ignored. This is what happened with Ogbu. Folks were too busy defending themselves and the great jobs we all were supposedly doing as parents that they couldn't pay attention to the more important problem still at hand—our underachieving children.

My husband is an only child because his parents wanted to give their child everything they never had, which was a lot. So in order to be able to fulfill that wish they decided to pour all their efforts into only one child. Most important on their list of things to give their son growing up in Pittsburgh was an education—the very best. So they sacrificed and saved and sent him clear across the blue-collar town to private school, making him a lone(ly) Black face in a sea of white privilege. At his prep school the students did not wear caps and gowns at graduation. Not at graduation from elementary school, not at junior high (or middle school in prep lingo), and not at their high school graduation, either. Instead they were required to wear dress shirts, ties, and jackets just as they did every day to class. The thinking was that the first time students should wear caps and gowns was the moment they graduated from college. And the expectation was that everyone at his prep school would certainly see that moment. These are expectations at their highest. I donned my first cap and gown when I "graduated" from Head Start.

It is irresponsible and overly simplistic to argue that there is some kind of correlation between the number of times we proudly watch our kids participate in the cap and gown march and achieving lasting success. And that is not what I am trying to do. In fact, I still haven't gotten over the guilt after recently missing my friend's daughter's graduation from preschool. But I do think there is something to expectations.

At my junior high school graduation the principal during his speech told us all to cherish the cap and gown moment because for some of us in the audience it would be our last graduation. It is the only moment of the entire graduation that I remember. That and the finger-lickin' dinner at Popeye's that my family inhaled afterward. (Yes we so ghetto.) At my next graduation, this time from high school, I couldn't stop hearing my old eighth-grade principal's words. There were indeed too many faces that were missing that night. My own boyfriend at the time, the son of a college professor, ended up being one of those who did not receive a high school diploma on graduation night.

Unfortunately, my boyfriend was not alone. A startling 2004 study by the Civil Rights Project at Harvard University and the Urban Institute concluded that only 50 percent of Black students graduate from high school and only 53 percent of Latino students are graduating from high school. For male students, the figures were even worse. Only 43 percent of Black males and 48 percent of Latino males graduated. Researchers concluded that the official data on dropout rates was misleading, arguing that in reality there are actually more dropouts than schools report. The study charged that school districts and states routinely try to depress their dropout numbers by pushing out and eliminating problem students from school rosters, especially right before state tests because higher scores translate into extra funding and certification credentials.[8] For instance, in many states students are removed from school rolls when they hit twenty-one regardless of whether they have received a diploma or not. Similarly, if they are incarcerated, they just cease to officially exist in school graduation data. In Texas, often hailed for its graduation rate success, students who for any reason cannot be accounted for, whether due to truancy or transfers, are removed from dropout calculations as if they never existed. Imagine the damage that would be done to Texas' stats if the true graduation status of these "missing persons" were figured in. In most states, students who say they left school for GED programs are not considered high school dropouts regardless of whether they actually receive their GED certificate or not. When researchers examine enrollment data instead of graduation records, comparing a school's freshmen figures to the size of the class when it graduates, dropout figures are much higher. In a study of the one hundred biggest school districts in the country, in almost half the schools sampled the size of the senior class had shrunk by more than half compared to the class size back in the ninth grade, four years earlier. In one year in Chicago 15,653 students graduated from high school while 17,404 students dropped out.[9] When it comes to Black students, New York is actually doing the worst. In New York only 35 percent of Black students graduate from high school (and 31 percent of Latino students). Back in 2001, five of the city's high schools actually discharged (erased from their rolls) more students than they graduated. The news prompted Advocates for Children of New York to file several federal class action lawsuits on behalf of New York's forgotten students, including a suit against Boys and Girls High.[10] In the Boys and Girls lawsuit filed in 2005 the school was accused of flagrantly pushing students out. The suit alleged that academically struggling students were housed in the auditorium for hours instead of being sent to class, thus ensuring that they would not earn the necessary credits for promotion. Then the students were told they could no longer attend the school.[11] Who knows what the true dropout rate of Boys and Girls High might really be?

Part of the Urban League's criticism of Ogbu's research was that he didn't pay enough attention to the expectations, specifically the low expectations that the district's white teachers may have had for their Black students. It is a delicate argument to make because there is no statistical measure for people's expectations. There are no numbers to point to, no surveys. Just judgments of behavior. Most people are not going to admit, even to themselves, that they may have low expectations. Hence the multitude of surveys that conclude with school-is-important results. But the same can be said for racism, or sexism, or any of the isms that plague society. Whether or not the ism is acknowledged depends on the perceptions and standards of the victim. Just because there isn't a viable measure doesn't mean there isn't something there to measure if we had the tools. Therefore there is no doubt in my mind that expectations carry a lot of weight.

High school students will not hesitate to tell you just that. A national survey conducted in 2005 of more than ten thousand teenagers found that 65 percent, or two of every three students, would work harder if their high school offered more demanding courses. Less than one in ten students said high school had been "very hard." In fact more than one-third said high school had been downright "easy."[12]

Chris, the double sophomore with the long line of exes, who was determined to graduate from high school no matter what his family thinks, didn't pass because he cut too much school. Instead of attending class he spent his days in the Internet café playing an online game called Guns against cyber-friends he'd never met. Since he was so determined to still graduate, even planning to take summer school and night school at one point to ensure that he could graduate on time, I had to ask him why he insisted on cutting so much school to begin with. "It's so easy," he said matter-of-factly. "It's so easy to slip by the guards at school. They don't care." Chris felt it was his obligation to leave school just because it was so easy to do so. "It is like the guards are begging us to." Don't the teachers say anything? "No." Parents? "My mom might ground me, but then the next day I go out and she doesn't say anything." Understandably, Chris had gotten very good at playing Guns but not so good at passing the tenth grade. And he is fulfilling everyone's expectations.

Pride can be a good thing, especially in a world that continues to ignore your achievements. It can even serve as a powerful survival tactic to stop you from being knocked down in the face of constant hurdles. But pride can also stifle success instead of propelling it. The danger of low expectations is that too much pride starts to pop up at the lowest accomplishments, the minimum of achievement, doing the bare minimum to move onward and upward. I wish young folks weren't satisfied simply because they managed to avoid summer school. Or just because they passed a test. Or according to Mama Johnson from the Rockaways, whose son is fond of setting the neighbors' Christmas wreaths ablaze, for not being "in the system." We are settling for rewards for taking a few beginning steps instead of finishing the race.

We, as a society, are living for the moment. Living for the moment is living without plans or a vision of tomorrow (so consequences don't matter) and without patience. (This should not be mistaken for living *in the moment*, or acknowledging and embracing all of life now, which for a community too often saddled with history can be quite healthy.) But this *for-the-momentness* shouldn't be news to anyone—the signs are all around us. Forget saving, credit cards allow us to buy what we want today. (The average person's credit card debt is about $9,000—more than four times what it was a decade ago.)[13] No need to diet, plastic surgery will make us all into swans immediately. (Gastric bypass surgery has increased 400 percent since 1999 when the singer Carnie Wilson had her stomach-stapling experience broadcast live on the Internet. There are now more than 140,000 such operations performed every year, and this procedure could soon be among the most common surgeries, surpassing prostate removal and hip replacement.)[14] News is twenty-four hours a day. Communication—e-mail, two-ways, text messages, cell phones—is instant. We don't even wait the nine months until our babies are born to find out the sex of our children anymore. (When I was pregnant, the minute I started showing, the first thing people would say was "Congratulations." The next was, "What are you having?" Then there was a moment of puzzlement when I explained that my husband and I were waiting to find out until our child was actually born. "Why?" my friend John kept asking.) Some psychologists have begun to argue that the lack of patience encouraged by instant gratification is so ingrained in children today that it is fueling their frustration and ultimately leading to more-violent children.[15]

My cousins, who seem to live quite nicely on government checks instead of paychecks, having everything from big-screen TVs with hundreds of channels to SUVs and booming stereo systems, love to point out how much more they have compared to the college-educated household of me and my husband. It is true. When it comes to toys, they often have the latest while we—juggling bills, college loans, and a mortgage—often feel like we are just getting by with the necessities.

The last time we went over to the cousins' house I saw the biggest TV I had ever seen in my life. It must have taken up half the living room. You could see it clearly from every corner of the main floor and probably even from across the street. Sitting on the oversized leather sectional, I tried to watch *Law & Order* once but Detective Briscoe's face was bigger than my entire body, making it difficult to concentrate. The *ba-dum-bump* in surround sound was also deafening. The house full of kids seemed to like it, though, so I was definitely in the minority. Of course, there are compromises necessary for such a lifestyle. We usually don't call the cousins because the telephone is constantly being disconnected. We've learned that, rather than keep track of the changing digits, it is easier to just wait for them to call us. One day we got a call from the cousins' house and the caller ID was in the baby's name, meaning the household's phone was registered with the telephone company to a nine-month-old. "His credit is the best." Not for long.

Their lives are ruled by the now. When they have a little bit of money in their pocket it is gone by the end of the weekend. Come Monday, empty pockets don't matter because it was a really good weekend.

The cousins are not alone. Honestly, most days I feel like there are probably more households like theirs than like mine. I can see all those big-screen TVs from across the street, down the block, and from the other side of town.

Yet the issues here are bigger than just wanting to enjoy the weekend. Because in order for the living-for-the-moment mentality to thrive, at some level you must believe that tomorrow can't possibly be better. So there is no need to prepare for Monday. Why work for tomorrow's moments if they probably won't be as good or may not come at all?

"What am I most proud of?" asks budding filmmaker Terrence, nineteen, of Bed-Stuy, repeating my question before spitting out, without a pause: "Being alive." Terrence has already seen eight of his friends, including Timothy, die from gun violence. "What am I most proud of? Being alive."

"What I want is for the kids to adopt better attitudes, to be engaged in class, to care about themselves and others, and to recognize and respect their own potential," says Patrick Welsh.[16]

Welsh is an English teacher at T. C. Williams High School in Alexandria, Virginia, a well-to-do suburb of historic town houses outside of Washington, D.C. T. C. is the school that Denzel Washington made famous in the Disney movie *Remember the Titans*. Denzel played the inspirational football coach of the school's first biracial team when it integrated in the 1970s. Welsh has been a teacher at T. C. for more than thirty years, long enough to teach some of the children of former students in his classroom. He came to my attention after he wrote an Op-Ed piece in the *Washington Post* under the headline "When the Street and the Classroom Collide." Welsh arrived at school one day to see a police car with flashing lights parked in the driveway and cops trying to break up a fight between two female students. He used this incident to discuss the tug-of-war at his suburban school between the thug mentality of the corner and the culture of the classroom. His words were so compelling in their familiarity and honesty that it was as if I had already met this teacher.

For Welsh, the most surprising thing about the police-car incident were the harsh criticisms of his own students, including high-achieving Black AP students, which he felt could have put Bill Cosby's class-laden rants to shame. His students summed up that morning's events in one word: "ghetto." "That's a word the kids use freely," he said. Welsh, a middle-aged white man, was actually startled by how frequently his students seemed to use the word that he had always felt was a bit taboo.

"I'm so embarrassed for them," says Dominique, one of Welsh's seniors who was on her way to attend Radford College in the fall, referring to her rowdier classmates. "They don't realize how ghetto they appear to others. They are desperate for attention. They think fighting is cute."[17]

The disdain dripping from Welsh's AP students is hard to miss. "Nothing frustrates me more than to see guys acting stupid to assure each other that they are Black," says Renee, complaining about the ghettoness of her younger brother, who refuses to speak proper English once he leaves the house.[18]

Welsh is a good teacher, so he hasn't given up hope . . . yet. Instead, he brings up a story about how two of his non-AP students felt compelled to come to his defense after some students outside his window started cursing him when he tried to get them to quiet down so he could teach. His two students instantly ran out of the classroom to "get" them. I guess the story is charming in a ghetto kind of way.

Although his students' hearts may have been in the right place, which is indeed a start, the image of two students running out of class to beat up a third made me realize how far we are from accomplishing Welsh's wish list. "What I want is for the kids . . .

> to adopt better attitudes,
> to be engaged in class,
> to care about themselves and others,
> and to recognize and respect their own potential."

T. C. High, which routinely sends students to the nation's best colleges, is that good suburban school that Boys and Girls High wishes it could be. T. C. is the only public high school in Alexandria, so, unlike much of our stratified school systems, it attracts a true diversity of academic and income levels. It is often compared to the best private schools because of its facilities and academics. For instance, T. C. is one of the only schools in Virginia that offers organic chemistry, a premed requirement in college. In the spring you can see T. C. students rowing on the Potomac River; the school, which has spawned several Olympic rowers, has the largest rowing team of any public school in the country. Alexandria also spends more money per student than any school system in the Washington, D.C., metropolitan area, and it recently became one of the first schools in the nation to provide laptops to all its students (the school campus has wireless Internet access).

Yet I couldn't get Boys and Girls High out of my mind when I started reading Welsh's words that day in the newspaper:

> A few weeks ago, I arrived at school to see a police car with flashing lights parked in the driveway. Nearby, two girls were rolling around on the ground, pummeling each other as a cop tried to pry them apart. One had threatened the other with a knife the night before, and now the girl who had been threatened was getting even with her fists.
>
> Meanwhile, the usual group of 15 to 20 guys were standing on the public sidewalk smoking and doing their best to affect the hard-core gangbanger thug look. They were dressed in the latest gangsta-rap attire: white T-shirts that come down to the knees and look like nightgowns, baggy jeans and assorted headgear. Some sported the popular throwback basketball jerseys that sell for at least $150, while others wore the cheaper ($75) Nike Swingman jerseys. Most were sporting the latest Jordan footwear, too.[19]

I've seen this very scene sitting outside Boys and Girls in the heart of Do-or-Die Bed-Stuy. I am not sure if our ghetto mentality started in places like Bed-Stuy and spread into larger society, infecting every cul-de-sac of Alexandria and beyond. Or if larger society, as a whole, changed first and our ghettoness is simply more magnified in communities like my beloved Bed-Stuy. I do know that once I started trying to write about Ghettonation, my few suburban friends who used to tease me a lot about my loyalty to Brooklyn interrupted their talk about their lawns, and their quiet towns, and how nice it all was for the children, and reluctantly started urging me to come out and talk to the teenagers in their suburbs, too. Now, after having done so, I tease my friends because "we all ghetto"—they just pay more taxes than I do to still be stuck living in it.

Why does ghetto have such pull? Why would kids going to a school rich enough to give them laptops still feel the need to thug it out on the corner or pull a knife on a classmate?

After being on the front lines of this tug-of-war day in and day out, Welsh, the teacher, had one conclusion: "T. C. is undeniably superb at controlling these kids so they don't run wild. But we're not so good at motivating them."

In the spring of 2006 the big-brain academics started to argue . . . in front of us, about this very question—the pull question. In newspaper Op-Ed pages and on talk radio, professors were bickering over the plight of Black men. They were in crisis! . . . the Ivy Tower realized, finally. A flurry of studies came out from the nation's top universities, including Harvard, Princeton, and Columbia, arguing that there were a whole lot of Black men out there who were disconnected from mainstream society. Sociologists and economists seemed stunned that in the 1990s (academics never talk about today; it is always yesterday), despite a booming economy, Black men fell further behind. Ronald Mincy, a big brain at Columbia and editor of *Black Males Left Behind*, one of the leading books that came out during this scholarly rush on the disconnected, argues that the same policy initiatives that helped bring poor Black women up the ladder had the opposite effect for Black men. In a nutshell, through welfare reform, $50 billion has been spent to require and enable young Black women to go to work. Tax credits then made low-wage work more profitable than welfare checks. Meanwhile their male counterparts did not get the same benefits. Stricter child support laws that garnished income often turned out to be economically stifling, in many cases putting men in debt and ultimately pushing some men to seek employment in that gray area of the economy because their earnings would be off the books and they could avoid having their wages garnished. Studies of employers also showed that the high incarceration rates of Black men negatively affected employment opportunities for all Black men.[20]

Amid the academic uproar, Orlando Patterson, a sociologist at Harvard, decided to veer in a different direction. He tried to argue culture. It was a culture of self-destructiveness that was holding these men back. According to Patterson, a so-called "cool-pose culture" that includes "hanging out on the street, dressing sharply, sexual conquests, party drugs, hip-hop music" was just too gratifying to give up. Culture was making the pull (of ghetto) attractive. "Not only was living this subculture immensely fulfilling," wrote Patterson in an Op-Ed piece in the New York Times. "It also brought them a great deal of respect from white youths."[21]

You could hear the collective gasp from liberal academics everywhere. Did one of our own just "blame the victim"? Gasp.

The gasps were so loud that people did not hear that Patterson's cultural explanation also included economics. Referencing the catchphrase from Bill Clinton's first presidential campaign, "It's the economy, stupid!" a host on NPR actually proved there is such a thing as a dumb question when she asked Patterson: "When it comes to young Black men, are you saying it's not the economy, it's the culture, stupid?" After a long moment the scholar stuttered to bring the conversation to an intelligent level: "I don't want to make it an either/or position," he said in his lilting Jamaican accent. "Economy is obviously important and always will be."[22]

In fact, Patterson has some interesting thoughts about the cycle of culture and economics. "You have this ironical situation where the kids who created the culture are being destroyed by the very culture which they created," argues Patterson. "At the same time it becomes part of the mainstream, even as they themselves are kept out of the mainstream by it."[23]

In other words: "Hip Hop, professional basketball, and homeboy fashions are as American as cherry pie," writes Patterson. "It has a powerful support from some of America's largest corporations."[24]

The professor's use of *homeboy* is probably proof enough that he hasn't spent much time lately on the corners that he thinks he is talking about. In fact, his definition of this insidious "culture" is problematic because he is leaning on the crutch that hip-hop equals all evil. And that is too easy. But even if the sloppy grouping of hip-hop, basketball, and homeboy doesn't make logical sense, on a gut level we understand what Patterson is trying to say. It is the ever-changing definition of ghetto that the scholar can't seem to define academically, but he feels it when he sees it. The danger with Patterson's cultural argument is that he doesn't seem to acknowledge that this culture is embraced not just by Black men. There are babymamas in Hollywood. In his own backyard, the college campus, instead of booty calls, white middle-class students are "hooking up."[25] And instead of forties, lacrosse* players are hugging beer kegs. (Ghetto)

What is more disappointing than the duh! conclusions of the research on the crisis among Black men is that solutions were hard to come by. Or when they were offered they were unsatisfying. In one radio interview, when asked directly what is the solution to this problem

---

* Thanks to Duke I now know that lacrosse exists, but I still don't know what the sport looks like.

of culture, Patterson fell silent. When he did gather his composure he sounded a lot like Mincy et al.—holding out policy as the answer. Mincy suggests that if it took $50 billion and years of initiatives to help dig Black men into this hole, then the same kind of effort needs to be introduced to help dig them out. To me it all sounded like a bunch of scholarly pipe dreams.

Still, I felt Patterson was on to something even if he couldn't pinpoint exactly what it was. The pull of ghetto cannot be attributed to just one narrow discipline. It is not just economics, just culture, just politics. If it were, finding the desperately needed fix would be easy. Therefore true solutions cannot and will not come from just one canon, either. Trying to crack the question of the pull of ghetto made me think of Gloria. When I met Gloria she was a six-figure executive doing HIV outreach for a major pharmaceutical company. She and her partner of twelve years were raising her two sons, a nephew, and a god-daughter in a cozy suburban home in Connecticut, a world away from the Brooklyn projects where she grew up. So picture-perfect was the home life of the two women, the only thing missing was the scent of cookies baking.

In the 1980s Gloria was a college-educated crackhead.

I interviewed her to write a feel-good magazine story about her triumph over addiction. About how she would leave her son and disappear for days, would hole up in abandoned buildings to get high. How she would resurface, her hair matted and dirty, staying home barely long enough to clean up before heading out again for another fix. How the girl voted most likely to succeed ended up on a dark Brooklyn corner with guns pointed at her head because she refused to give up her stash.

"One of the things drugs did to me was they took my dreams away. I finally feel like I can dream again," said Gloria after fifteen years of being clean. As she shared her addiction story, I didn't feel so good. I couldn't stop thinking about Ghettonation. It occurred to me, for the first time, that maybe ghetto is an addiction. That would explain why the pull is so strong.

Gloria continued to share, and like a friend I sat at the edge of my seat and rocked slightly, too eager for more. With this lightbulb suddenly shining over my head, I had to hear every last word. "Dreaming is okay," she continued. "I don't want people to give up on that. Sometimes dreams change, but dreaming is very important."

The last time I talked to Gloria she was thinking about applying to a PhD program in social work. She wants to study breaking the cycle of addiction in families. "We have all these cycles that we just continue to spin around because we are so comfortable," Gloria observed. "I don't want my kids," she paused, "to be that comfortable."

Gloria probably has no idea how much she helped me on my ghetto journey. As excited as I was about her revelations, part of me felt heavy from the insight. Addictions are hard to break. Even if you are strong enough to shed the behavior, you may never shed the taste. Just ask someone who has ever puffed on a cigarette.

Gloria is right about dreaming, though. Ghetto, like drugs, can steal your dreams away.

. . .

The no-hope syndrome—thinking tomorrow could be worse—was still bothering me. I couldn't get proud-to-be-alive Terrence out of my head.

Dr. Todd Boyd says it's the times. The USC professor reminded me that I have not been paying attention to history when he suggested it is all about the times. "People in the seventies were the first generation to participate in a society where Black people were no longer bound by the rules of segregation, so there was still a sense of hope amidst all the despair," said Dr. B., trying to set me straight during that last reality check of mine. "The hip-hop generation came of age when hope had given way to the harsh realities of a deteriorating urban core, high unemployment, crack cocaine, and the prison industrial complex, and so aggression and nihilism grow out of these specific conditions."

Makes sense. New research on mobility, the official term for moving up and down the economic ladder, shows there is actually far less of it than economists once thought, and even less than most people believe. There are signs that mobility has flattened or even declined recently. Fewer families moved up in the eighties than in the seventies, and even fewer moved up in the nineties than in the eighties. Now researchers say the economic advantage that they thought lasted two or three generations really lasts closer to five. The meritocracy that helps us believe tomorrow could be better may not be the playing field–leveler that we had hoped. Although we are a nation that proudly boasts that merit is the determining factor for success, that so-called merit, it turns out, is at least partly class based. A weeklong series on class in America put together by a team of reporters at the *New York Times* argued: "Parents with money, education and connections cultivate in their children the habits that the meritocracy rewards." These habits are what we generally think of as traditional middle-class values and behavior—from dress, to language, to affiliations, tastes, education, and experiences. The report concluded: "When their children then succeed, their success is seen as earned."[26] If fewer folks are actually climbing the ladder, then it means ghetto, the mind-set, can be crippling.

The part of Ogbu's thesis that still strikes a chord with me is that if we are to blame, even partly, then that is something we have the power to fix. Racism, the systemic faults of our school systems, even the expectations of others, are all ongoing, long-term problems. Yet our own expectations, which include not only what we expect from our kids, their expectations of themselves, and what we expect to bring to the table, as in school involvement, are something we can control, work at, and, most important, raise.

And if those expectations ever rise high enough, then maybe I'll be able to send my own child to Boys and Girls High, with pride and joy.

Celebs Make It Too Easy

Some things need no explanation.

Knowing every verse of R. Kelly's "Trapped in the Closet" (parts 1 to whatever)

Being Bobby Brown, the series and the real life

Lil' Jon and the East Side Boyz

DJ Cash Money (Birdman and Friends)

The fact that Jesse Jackson has a love child

BET

During the E! live red-carpet Oscar pre-show, Harvard-educated actress Natalie Portman yucks it up with Star Jones about how "empowering" her pole-dancing workout is. The two conclude that every woman should take a pole-dancing class.

Crunk Energy Drink, Pimp Juice, Chronic 187 Soda

G-Unit watches (complete with "iced spinners" courtesy of Jacob the Jeweler)

Paramount Pictures' original billboards for the movie *Get Rich or Die Tryin'* featured the bare, tattooed back of 50 Cent, his arms outstretched in full crucifixion pose, his head adorned with the do-rag/baseball cap combo. He clutches a mike in one hand and a gun in the other. As if the image wasn't ghetto enough, the movie studio placed the billboards near schools in gang-ridden areas, prompting the non-ghetto response of parent protests across the country.

The Irv Gotti trial. After a federal grand jury acquitted the hip-hop impresario and his brother of using their record label, Murder Inc., to launder drug money, two women on the jury asked that the brothers be brought into the jury room, where they then hugged them. The hugging continued when the brothers—who legally changed their surname to Gotti—jumped on a table in the courtroom to hand out hugs and shout-outs to some of their artists in the courtroom, including Ja Rule. That night the Gotti brothers and Murder Inc. crowd threw a victory bash on a large yacht docked in the Hudson River where guests, including Russell Simmons, walked around the deck in their socks, ate Ray's pizza, smoked, and drank the night away.

8
COS SPEAKS

In the spring of 2004 all this ghetto madness finally caused someone who white folks care about to lose his mind. (Up in here! Up in here!)

It was Bill Cosby.

Accepting an award from the NAACP during a bourgie dinner celebrating the fiftieth anniversary of *Brown v. Board of Education*, TV-land's überdad did what parents have to do sometimes—he gave the polite crowd (and the rest of us) a spanking.

It came in the form of an angry rant wherein Cos, unfortunately, picked on the easiest and safest of targets—the poorest among us. "Ladies and gentlemen," he began, "the lower economic and lower-middle-economic people are not holding up their end in this deal." He then went off on the "Shaniquas, the Shaliguas, the Mohammeds and all that crap." And he had some great one-liners, too (he is, after all, a comedian): "Five or six different children—same woman, eight, ten different husbands or whatever. Pretty soon you're going to have to have DNA cards so you can tell who you're making love to."[1]

The crowd of Black bourgeoisie cheered, erupting in applause fifteen different times during the meandering speech. The cheering spread to college campuses, Black intellectual circles, and professional groups. I got wind of Cosby's cause first through e-mail. Snippets from his NAACP speech were quickly forewarded through the Black Web gossip mill and landed in my inbox shortly after leaving his lips. The Amens, the Thank-Yous, the LOLs, could be heard around the world.

The issue spread to the white media, too. Lending their support were CNN, *Nightline*, NPR, and others, all allowing Cosby to hold court, often in sweats and sunglasses, giving him one of the best weapons to attack his own people—a mike. And the applause even spread to the presidential campaign. At a national convention of journalists of color that year, presidential candidate John Kerry was asked about Cosby's assessment that some Black folks were not pulling their weight. "I understand exactly where Bill is coming from with his comments," Kerry told the crowd. "He is right. People in the community need to take responsibility. But we need to do things as a society because all of us are responsible."

More surprising than the fact that the question was asked at all (to the horror of some who saw the issues as a private family dispute) was that a presidential candidate actually answered. He answered the question, without hesitation, because it never was a private family dispute. The issues of Ghettonation have become that universal.

For the first time that I could remember, Cosby reminded me of someone in my own family. I didn't know any Cliff Huxtables growing up, not even close. But the fed-up Cosby was much more real to me. His rant—inaccuracies, misstatements, the long windy tangents, and all—sounded like something my dad could have said if he were still around today. Or my Uncle Bugs, who can still hold your attention effortlessly by talking for an hour without even taking a breath. With his brilliant conspiracy logic, Uncle Bugs's rants could connect the neighborhood's unemployment rate to the White House to the war to missing the bus that morning. So Cosby's rant at that NAACP dinner sounded familiar. It was that talk of older Black men—Pops, rather Mr.

Pops (respect, of course)—who are at that point where they say whatever is on their mind and don't care what anyone thinks. I often wish we had all reached that point.

Truth is, Cosby's anger is misdirected. His frustration is not really with those "lower economic people" but with ghetto, as in the mindset. That is what Cosby is describing when he talks about families with multiple babydaddies, schools that are sending more students to jail than to college, and materialistic consumption rather than wealth building—none of which is restricted to class. Cosby, who more recently has been battling charges that he drugged and groped several women, is proof of that. Ghetto strikes us all.

It's too easy to blanketly-blame an entire class rather than to actually pick out the bad apples—wherever they fall. That was Cosby's biggest mistake. And understanding that the problem is much deeper than just "those people," whoever they may be, is the most important and the hardest step to recovery.

Despite the faults of Cosby's rant, what can't be ignored is the anger that overflows from all of us who nodded and applauded. Anger that comes from being frustrated and fed up and utterly at a loss to make some sense of how we got to this point. The anger that comes from being forced to wonder: why we gotta be like that? Cosby got us talking out loud about it, instead of tsk-tsking under our breath (ghetto); it became clear that the anger and frustration were already widespread.

"We have got to do something," David, a fortysomething power-to-the-people Black marketing entrepreneur pleaded with me over the phone one day. His exasperation was deafening. We were strangers then; it was about five minutes into our first conversation. David was in marketer mode trying to pitch me, the journalist, grand ideas about spreading the "positive message" of a recent story I had written about Black corporate pioneers. He particularly wanted young people to know about the unsung civil rights heroes. "My son is a freshman in college and I look at these young people . . . ," his voice trailed off. "We," he begged, "have . . . got . . . to . . . do . . . something!"

Almost a year after the NAACP gala, I was suffering from morning sickness while uncomfortably sitting on stage at the Schomburg Center for Research in Black Culture with some fellow Black authors as part of a panel discussion related to Cosby's mouth-off. The panel was part of the Harlem Book Fair—an annual block par-tay devoted to books.

As I looked out from the stage, I couldn't believe the auditorium was full. I had been to the fair before and had always stuck to the scene outside, skimming through tables of books in the summer sunshine. Most fairgoers like to get their books signed by authors who are making appearances at tables throughout the day. For me, just seeing folks, Black folks, stand in line to buy books was enough excitement. That morning, there I was with an auditorium full of people who preferred to be inside with us rather than out with the par-tay. What were they expecting? I was a little nervous. I was sure if I relaxed, even for a moment, my growing round belly would just tip my exhausted body right off the stage.

Inspired by Cosby's rant, us talking heads were trying to make sense of the "class divide in Black America," otherwise known as The Gap. Sitting at my right was Michael Eric Dyson. The event was his moment. The prolific writer had just released a book in record speed to respond to Cosby and thus dominated the discussion. While Dyson was busy blasting the comedian's infamous speech for its classist elitism, the rest of the panel, as well as the audience, were busy nodding in agreement with differing degrees of conviction. The parroting was stunning. Since Cos uttered his first angry words, I had never encountered a group that seemed less enthusiastic about his message. I didn't really buy it, though. When Cosby first erupted I had already started on this book. As a proud Black woman, I'd been obsessed with the epidemic of ghettoitis for a while. I had talked to enough people before, during, and after the speech to know that there was this underlying frustration and that a lot of people understood exactly where Cosby was coming from, even if some among them were careful not to applaud his classist rhetoric. The audience's reluctance to fully voice that frustration that day at the Schomburg Center I saw as a credit to Dyson's ability to lead and a sign of the power of group thought. I sat silent that day, too.

To me, most of the discussion that morning had missed the point. No reasonable person would support a solely class-based attack. Yet there is a difference between ghetto and class. And in Cosby's frustrated soul, I have to believe ghetto is really what Mr. Pops was blasting. At his best, Cosby tried to challenge those of us who thought we were doing everything right, as opposed to simply inviting us to criticize those we think are doing all wrong.

"Brown versus the Board of Education is no longer the white person's problem," Cosby chastised. I nodded and agreed. "We've got to take the neighborhood back. We've got to go in there," he demanded. I agreed, again. "Just forget telling your child to go to the Peace Corps. It's right around the corner. It's standing on the corner. It can't speak English. It doesn't want to speak English. I can't even talk the way these people talk." I could hear and feel the class snobbery, yet after months of standing on the corner with my notebook, I couldn't stop myself from giggling.

"I'm telling you Christians, what's wrong with you?" Cosby pleaded. This was getting good, I thought. The wagging finger was turning inward. "Why can't you hit the streets?" he wagged. "Why can't you clean it out yourselves?" he wagged, again. "It's our time now, ladies and gentlemen. It is our time. And I've got good news for you. It's not about money. It's about you doing something ordinarily that we do—

get in somebody else's business. It's time for you to not accept the language that these people are speaking, which will take them nowhere. What the hell good is *Brown v. Board of Education* if nobody wants it?"[2]

When Cosby was done with his Mr. Pops rant, amid the cheers, some folks soon started accusing the comedian of airing dirty laundry. In response to the criticisms he did what my dad would do; he refused to shush, and instead got louder.

"Let me tell you something," Cosby shot back during a Rainbow PUSH event several weeks after his speech, with Jesse Jackson nodding his head in support, "your dirty laundry gets out of school at 2:30 every day, it's cursing and calling each other nigger as they're walking up and down the street. They think they're hip. They can't read; they can't write. They're laughing and giggling, and they're going nowhere." We cheered again.

I admit it, the dirty-laundry comment was my favorite of Cos's sound bites. It still makes me chuckle. (I be ghetto.) In the spirit of airing dirty laundry, I must say that I have always felt that part of what also drives this generation of Black professionals to succeed so strongly is the (unconscious) desperate need to differentiate themselves from ghetto because this generation is more closely tied to that ghetto world than perhaps any talented tenth before. While there is still indeed a Black aristocracy—bourgie Black folk who have been at the top for generations—there are also Black climbers now, those who, despite the proven mobility ceilings, have been able to climb from one class to the next thanks to the death of Jim Crow and the gains of the civil rights movement. It is among these straddlers, like myself, where ghetto is often so obviously very close to home. We commonly have one foot in and one foot out. Our family is full of both kinds: those who made it out and those who are still stuck in. We are embarrassed by ghetto, not because it is so unfamiliar but because it is too familiar. And without the financial safety net that a long line of Bourgie heritage provides, we can be one paycheck away from falling back where we started.

As someone who straddles both worlds every day, a Black professional in a white office but one who still lives in the hood (and is often more comfortable at home than at work), when Cosby exploded, I felt the finger being wagged, even if I embraced what he was saying. He was talking about my neighbors, my family, the world I gladly go home to every night. For me the issues weren't ever *those* people but *my* people.

"We're getting judged for half of the population," says Eric, twenty, standing on Martin Luther King Boulevard in the middle of the workday in Dallas. "Everybody doesn't behave like that. I was always taught that you don't judge a book by its cover, that you have to open it up and read it first. Seems like Cosby is judging all young people by the cover."[3]

No doubt. That's why John and his wife, Deborah, college professors cushioned by the theoretical world of academics, always assumed that I saw Cosby's rant for all its elitism. "She's going to blast Cosby" is how Deb, rolling her eyes when she said *Cosby*, proudly described the work she thought I was doing. It wasn't that easy, though. I found that my emotions—my anger, frustration, annoyance, and disgust—proved more convincing than what my mind knew was logical, or even right. Those why-we-gotta-be-like-*that* moments were stopping me from fully blasting Cosby as Deb hoped I would.

Eric's idealism is envious. I guess I'm too grown up not to ignore that we live in a country where covers often *do* carry more weight.

Robert Carmona's solution is "squaring up." Carmona is an ex-heroin addict who spent his early twenties in and out of jail. After being arrested on a robbery charge he avoided a five-year sentence by agreeing to enter a two-year rehab program. "I didn't really go in to change. I just didn't want to go to jail," admits Carmona. But he did change. When he was released, he was clean for the first time in years, yet still he couldn't find a job. He took action. In 1985 he started STRIVE (Support and Training Result in Valuable Employees) in the basement of the public housing project in East Harlem where he grew up. The non-profit, devoted to giving job training to society's most difficult to employ—former drug addicts, ex-cons, lifetime welfare recipients—now has offices in nineteen cities, including London. The tough-love program focuses on soft interpersonal skills, such as culture and dress, that Carmona felt would have helped him not only get a job but keep a job when he was trying to turn his life around. "The world may be tougher for a Black guy than a white guy, but I keep telling them that we tend to hurt ourselves more than the world can," says Carmona, who dishes out no sugar when he speaks. "You have to be squaring up."[4] The program is free, but participants are fined each time they do not meet expectations and break the rules. Using slang (50 cents), not wearing nametags ($1.50), late for class (grounds for termination). STRIVE has a class on shedding the "game face"—the hard, don't-mess-with-me look that is too common among young men around the way. Carmona likes to talk about "code switching" as he bluntly encourages young men to drop the game face for job interviews and the workplace. James, thirty, of Brooklyn, who looks like he has never cracked a smile, admits the "game face" is unconscious. "But, I'm trying to square up."[5] Another class on fatherhood centers on discussions of what it means to be a man. "When do we learn to own our stuff?" Carmona challenges a room full of job seekers on their first day of the monthlong boot camp program. "Square up!"[6] Since his nonprofit started back in that East Harlem basement, STRIVE has placed more than 25,000 people, mostly Black and Latino men, in jobs, and more than 70 percent are still employed after two years.

Learning to navigate different worlds is necessary for survival. And it is something Ghettonation too often forgets. Square up!

At its crux, Cosby's point was very simple. He was complaining about parenting rather than the lack of parenting. I cannot help but agree that parenting behavior needs to be changed.

You got to tell me that if there was parenting—help me—if there was parenting, he wouldn't have picked up the Coca-Cola bottle and walked out with it to get shot in the back of the head. He wouldn't have. Not if he loved his parents. And not if they were parenting! Not if the father would come home. Not if the boy hadn't dropped the sperm cell inside of the girl and the girl had said, "No, you have to come back here and be the father of this child." Not . . . "I don't have to."[7]

Whenever the worst ghetto moments pop up, Roy, an adoptive father, often argues that all parents should have to go through the preparation and screening that he and his wife had to go through before they were allowed to adopt. Indeed, anyone who has hit puberty can make a baby; it takes so much more to become a parent, though. The reality-TV craze chronicling our children's bad behavior, from shows like *SuperNanny* to *Brat Camp*, is proof that we have gotten to the point that our shoddy parenting skills are considered entertaining.

The fact that we all may be bad parents is not an excuse, though. It is like failing a test and arguing that the whole class failed. So what? I knew better than to try that line in my house growing up. Like shooting bullets at Superman, such an excuse would simply bounce off my mom, who would shoot back one of her crippling looks of disapproval and administer the "If everyone jumped off the Brooklyn Bridge" speech. ("If everyone jumped off the Brooklyn Bridge, would you jump, too?" "No, ma'am.")

The reality that never makes it to TV is that there are more than 540,000 children neglected in this country every year. That does not include serious physical, mental, or sexual abuse, which brings the total to just under 1 million kids.[8] Instead more than 540,000 children fall under the government's definition of neglect, meaning the "deprivation of *adequate* food, clothing, shelter, or medical care for no apparent financial reason."[9] Or simply, kids who exist without basic parenting. And those are by government standards. Now imagine how high the numbers would be if we included mothers lacking common sense, deadbeat fathers, what-are-they-thinkin'? folks, the un-caregivers feeding their kids soda-filled bottles, the knuckleheads cussing at their toddlers, and all the rest of the plain old *bad* parents. The number of children that we neglect is, well, nothing less than astronomical.

That day when Cosby lost his mind, one fed-up Mr. Pops who was up in there was the activist, comedian, and health-food guru Dick Gregory. At the *Brown v. Board of Ed* gala in Washington, it was Gregory who presented Cosby with an NAACP award that night. (After all, that was why Cosby was there, to be honored for the millions he has donated to Black colleges over the years.) After Cosby's caustic remarks, Gregory jokingly ran up to his longtime friend and pretended to steal his medal as if to imply that the classist rant made him unworthy of the honor. "This is what happens when they get old," Cosby joked about Gregory.

It is a bit ironic that it was Cosby's words instead of something Gregory might have said that actually got the people's tongues wagging. Gregory, in contrast to Cosby, has never just told jokes. While Cosby built his career as a crossover comedian, one of the first to successfully figure out how to make Black *and* white faces laugh, Gregory was the in-your-face Black comedian who never let you forget he was Black first. Heavily immersed in the civil rights movement, Gregory delivered comedy that was always smart, political, and racially conscious. That's a little different from hawking Jell-O Pudding Pops.

In the late 1950s, Gregory was doing stand-up gigs at night in small Black nightclubs for so little money that he had to work at the post office full-time during the day. Hugh Hefner caught his act and booked him at the Playboy Club in Chicago. At his first show at the Playboy Club in December 1961, not only was the audience 100 percent white, it was filled with Southerners in for a convention. Unfazed, Gregory took the stage at the bunny club and opened with

> Good evening ladies and gentlemen. I understand there are
> a good many Southerners in the room tonight. I know the
> South very well. I spent twenty years there one night. Last
> time I was down South I walked into this restaurant and this
> white waitress came up to me and said, "We don't serve col-
> ored people here." I said, "That's all right. I don't eat colored
> people. Bring me some fried chicken." Then these three
> white boys came up to me and said, "Boy, we're givin' you
> fair warnin'. Anything you do to that chicken, we're gonna
> do to you." So I put down my knife and fork, I picked up
> that chicken and I kissed it. Then I said, "Line up, boys!"[10]

That was his introduction to the white world. With his edgy social criticism, Gregory brought down the house, and Hef offered him a job, giving the comedian national exposure that forever changed the face of American comedy. "From that moment," *Newsweek* wrote, "the Jim Crow school of humor was dead." The door had been opened for the likes of Redd Foxx, Richard Pryor, Paul Mooney, Chris Rock, Dave Chappelle, and Bill Cosby.

Even from the beginning, Gregory was a frontline activist. Speaking out against the Vietnam War, marching for civil rights, embracing Stokely Carmichael. In 1968 Gregory even ran for president as a write-in candidate. On his Web site, which is a mix of his radical musings, Afrocentric news and links, and health dogma (Gregory adheres to a strict diet of only fruit and raw foods that he claims cured his cancer), there is an undated photo of him being led away in handcuffs during some kind of protest. The photo's caption reads: "I will go to jail for you. What will you go for?"

I heard Dick Gregory ranting once about one of my favorite ghetto pet peeves—the use of the phrase "the N-word." I find this PC term even more offensive than the word it replaces because it devalues language. By using a substitute, it's like trying to make acceptable something that has no business being so. In that way, using "N-word" is no different from (and no less ghetto than) when the hip-hop generation uses *nigga.* Apparently Gregory thinks so, too. "Can you imagine if Jews changed 'concentration camps' to 'the C-word'?" he asked a hotel ballroom of Black journalists during a recent convention in Atlanta. His white fro and shaggy beard created a halo that contrasted comfortably with his aged brown face. (My dad and Uncle Bugs, in Mr. Pops tradition, have sported that halo, too.) "The word is *nigger!*" he said, spitting out the syllables with the full hatred with which the word is supposed to be uttered. "Changing that to 'the N-word' changes history!" Then, proof that the comedian had never really disappeared, he couldn't resist and added: "I say 'nigger' every morning to keep my teeth white." The audience couldn't resist and laughed.

So that it was Cosby and not Gregory who created such a controversy at the NAACP gala was a bit surprising. After his friend lost his mind, Gregory danced the awkward middle between not exactly blasting Cosby while not exactly embracing his old friend, either.

"There's ten thousand compassionate ways he could have said what he said," says Gregory. "Of course there's a problem facing Black youth, but there's a problem facing America. There's problems with education, there's problems with drugs, there's problems with television violence. If Blacks are on the lowest rung of the social and economic ladder, of course we're going to suffer more."[11]

Indeed, something's out of whack. My journeys tell me so: witness the Apple Bottoms Mr. Softee truck, Red-T's subway fun, the Boys and Girls High, the sixteen exes, the Adalia Johnsons. But what disturbs me most these days is what *we* are doing to ourselves—that is, what we can control. That by no means implies that there are not very traceable and deliberate reasons, policies, actions, even vast conspiracies from either wing, that have created the situations that we are now struggling to overcome. Those same forces don't care if we ever get up. I am not the first to say that we need to start climbing and pulling and pushing each other up ourselves. Yet apparently the message needs repeating.

The danger when you start to focus on self-responsibility is that it lets others off the hook. The in-house bickering not only sucks energy away from common enemies but also offers those mastering the isms— racism, sexism, homophobia, and whatever else—the perfect excuse to support their discrimination. Cosby's class snobbism, stereotypes, and sloppy facts are great ammunition for the other side. But the advantage of cleaning up our own act is the strength that can be gained when we stop holding ourselves down. Imagine how much better we will then be able to fight. And in that vein I think my dad, Uncle Bugs, Dick Gregory, and the rest of the tell-it-like-it-is fed-up Mr. Popses everywhere would agree, some things just need to be said.

Cosby ended his speech how he began, with a little sarcasm, a little humor, and a little finger-wagging. Most important, he ended it with a challenge:

> Well, you're probably going to let Jesus figure it out for you.
> Well, I've got something to tell you about Jesus. When you
> go to the church, look at the stained-glass things of Jesus.
> Look at them. Is Jesus smiling? Not in one picture. So, tell
> your friends. Let's try to do something. Let's try to make
> Jesus smile. Let's start parenting.[12]

The challenge wasn't to "those people." He stared out from the podium onto that middle-class crowd and challenged *all* of us to do better.

No one seems to remember that part.

That's so ghetto . . .

Add your own *"Why we gotta be like that?"* moments here. To see what other readers have come up with and add to Ghettonation's ever-growing *That's so ghetto* list, send to www.coradaniels.com/ghettolist.

9

DO YOU SPEAK?

Ghetto used to be a more negative term, now it depends on
the context. Good or bad, I try not to use the word a lot.

—AISHA, EIGHTEEN, BROOKLYN

I began this journey in hopes of letting Ghettonation speak. My first discovery was that everyone
thinks they know ghetto. My second was that folks
had a lot to say about it. It seems that there is a lot
of "sick and tired" going around. Of all those trying
to get things off their frustrated chests, Vanessa
stood out. The mere mention of *Ghettonation* put
the publicist and promotions manager into fits of
laughter for hours. My favorite of Vanessa's get-it-
off-her-chest moments was the one about the
woman with the money manicure.

Vanessa knows Sandra tangentially—she's a friend or acquaintance
of a friend or an acquaintance several times removed. Every so often
their paths do cross. One night they met during an old-fashioned girls'
night of food and all-night talk at the home of a friend. Sandra arrived
late because she had just had her nails done, and she strolled in flashing the chedda. Literally. Nine of her nails had bits of a $20 bill embed-

ded in the polish. The tenth nail had a picture of Beyoncé's face. Vanessa couldn't take her eyes off those nails. I had never even met Sandra, but hearing about her, I couldn't shake the image, either.

By the way, Sandra is sixty-two years old.

The grandmother and her nails often dip into Vanessa's thirtysomething circles because of the men Sandra dates—always much younger and always hot. As the girls' night wore on and the drinks and snacks settled in, the conversation turned, as it always does, to men. Sandra was pissed. She was going through a breakup. Her man had just left her for another woman, she said. Hisses and supportive groans circled the room as Sandra complained about "the bitch who stole her man." (Nails aside, placing all the blame on the other woman instead of portioning out some for her lying, cheating man is what clinched Sandra's ghetto status for me.)

"If I see her, I am going to beat her down," said Sandra to a rumbling of "You go, girl" and "I got your back" support. She waved her $20-bill-laden nails back in acknowledgment.

Truth is, Sandra wasn't really that torn up about the breakup. Turns out her boyfriend's biggest flaw was his age. At only eighteen years younger than she, he had gotten too old, she complained. She was already getting nibbles from a younger, more desirable catch. Still, the room could taste the beat-down blood and had already worked itself into a frenzy over "seeing the bitch" scenarios. As Vanessa grew tired of the posturing, she asked Sandra why she didn't just let it go.

"Because . . . I'm a woman of my word," Sandra said with the serious sincerity that comes with surviving sixty-two years. "And if I see her I will . . . beat . . . her . . . down."

As Vanessa finished her story about Sandra, the room listening to her during my own girls' night could think of nothing to say.

And that, I realized, is really the point.

After talking about all things ghetto for months and months—exposing stories about money manicures, ice cream trucks with booming systems, tall Ts, do-rags, and tight tops that read TOO SEXY and JUICY, children who wave guns in fake stickups and man-boys waving real guns to "make us do anything," babydaddies, on-the-side confessions, and back-that-ass-up dance recitals, after *nigga* this and *nigga* that, Head Start graduations, and didyapass? congrats—after months of low expectations, I have come to realize that it is that silence that says more than all of the discussions.

Silence is our downfall.

I was eight months pregnant and waddling to the hospital for an appointment as fast as I could through the streets of Brooklyn. The belly drew attention, and I had gotten used to the stares and the smiles. I took the opportunity to stare back and not hide my natural eavesdropping tendencies. In one of those nosey moments I saw her T-shirt first before anything else. It was black and tight (of course) and in silver sparkly script it spelled out GHETTO BABY across her chest. The sparkle shined even more brightly than expected because the black T was paired with black pants and black sneakers. In fact, the entire crowd of young men and women on the corner was draped in black—jeans, T-shirts, bandannas, caps, and sneakers. Except for the GHETTO BABY message it was an uninterrupted sea of black from head to toe, about twenty-five people deep. Some in the group were leaning against a mammoth black SUV with black tinted windows, smoking cigarettes. As I tried to squeeze through the crowd, as far away from the secondhand Newport menthol smoke as I could get, I practically stepped into the open storefront doorway to my side. There was a buzz of activity as folks were zipping back and forth from the curb to the entrance. That is when I noticed that this group of young folks, in their black jeans, black dorags, and black Ts, were gathered in front of a funeral home. With their typical "game face" stares replaced with grief, they looked so young. I must have been older than every face there by about a decade. The last thing I spotted was the back window of the black SUV. There was a message neatly printed in white where you'd usually see JUST MARRIED. Instead it read R.I.P. BENJIE. The young woman with the GHETTO BABY T and her young friends were burying one of their own. I crossed the avenue and stroked my belly. My baby was kicking wildly. I couldn't help but smile thinking of what grandmama&em used to say about when one spirit leaves this world, another is born.

The time has come for the death of ghetto. That is why I sat down to write these last 182 pages.

Amid all the assumptions people made about what Ghettonation must be, what stood out is that everyone was convinced they knew what ghetto meant. They were eager to rattle off their endless pet peeves, wag their fingers, and drive themselves into fits of nervous laughter over "why we gotta be like that?" moments. But no one in all those conversations ever offered a cure. "Solution?" Vanessa asked, puzzled. "What solution?"

When the great American architect I. M. Pei came to Bed-Stuy, he gave up, too. In 1966, Bed-Stuy became a national symbol of urban despair after New York senator Robert F. Kennedy took an infamous tour of the neighborhood and then called on Congress to help save it. Out of legislation written by Kennedy and fellow New York senator Jacob Javits, the nation's first nonprofit community development organization was created to revive the neighborhood. At the time Pei was called upon to help rehabilitate the area. He turned the job down. "Like most ghettos, Bedford-Stuyvesant has no focus," he said. "There are endless streets leading from nowhere to nowhere."[1] The architect could have been speaking only about design. But the description resonates more than thirty years later because it speaks to so much more. Ghetto has no focus. It is like being on a path that leads from nowhere to nowhere. Pei was absolutely right.

I'm not ready to throw up my hands and accept that there is no solution. Or walk away from the job. My expectations are higher. The words of Daniel, the budding filmmaker who still has hope, are still ringing in my head: "We are not a lost cause." He is right, too. Mindsets *can* be broken.

When Saint Jill (Nelson) was speaking up about pimps and ghetto Oscars after the awards show, she also had something to say about giving up. She blames her generation, those who came of age in the sixties and seventies, for being so heartbroken that they clammed up. "We watched Malcolm and Robert Kennedy die and by the time they took Martin we gave up," says Nelson. "We lost hope." Nelson argues that because her generation went through so much pain in their quest for systematic change, they then turned around and tried to shield their children from any pain. "We smothered our kids in material stuff to insulate them from the pain," she says. White people aware enough to be involved in the movement went back to their tranquil lives, and those Black people who could, entered into the middle class to relish some of that tranquility. "We dropped the ball. We did not pass on to our kids the struggle that we went through." Speak up! Speak up!*

It wasn't the first time that I had heard the theory. In fact, just a few weeks after that post-Oscar conversation, I found myself at a national function of Black marketers at which a senior Mr. Pops bent my ear for a good twenty-five minutes with his thoughts along the same lines. His solution was to build a museum, something he was trying to do in his hometown of Philly, dedicated to our most painful images starting with slavery. In fact, he argued that the history of Black people in this country is marked by several periods of slavery (if not literal, then psychological), each followed by a period of violence. (I think we are supposedly in the slave cycle now. Or maybe it is violence. I can't remember, for

---

* By the way, Nelson also speaks up on the subway, telling teenagers to refrain from using *nigger* or *motherfucker* until after she gets off. She hasn't gotten a refusal yet.

sure—funny how both seem appropriate these days.) However, when Nelson spoke up that day it was the first time I had heard someone from that generation admit that the theory that we have dropped the ball could be valid. I took the assertion that we should take responsibility as a sign that recovery was indeed possible.

My journeys started with Bed-Stuy, and that is where they end. Asked about her take on ghetto, Aisha, of the "successful family," sucked in her teeth in true around-the-way BK disgust. "I just don't think anyone should be called ghetto," she told me. As someone who is driven every day (who am I kidding, every hour) to call someone or something I see ghetto, I immediately felt a tinge of shame over my addictive dependence on the characterization. Aisha, a child of Bed-Stuy lifers and proud of her Bed-Stuy roots, is weary of stereotypes, though, especially since she feels that as soon as she says where she's from, stereotypes—the ghetto kind—are usually thrown her way. "I try not to use the word," she told me.

I was impressed with Aisha's BWL Whatism insight. It is easy to wag our fingers and call someone ghetto. It is much harder to recognize ghetto in ourselves. Too many times Aisha has seen how ghetto has been dished out hypocritically. I don't think that I'm ready to abandon the use of ghetto. The mind-set is indeed there. Yet the advantage to Aisha's solution is that it may help us to stop seeing ghetto only in those who are most obviously ailing.

By the time Vanessa finished getting all those moments off her chest, my sides hurt from giggling so hard. As predicted in the beginning of my journeys, we did talk about nails, and gold teeth, about weaves—blond and red—about baby bottles filled with Pepsi, about babymamas, and about all things Crunk. And for the night, with our laughter, the small group of us in my basement had managed to block out all sounds of Brooklyn, even the thought police. Our squeals made us feel like teenagers again, and we held our sides because they hurt. My husband, who had never been subjected to such a girlfest before, was awkwardly crossing his legs and almost hopping like little boys do when the laughing becomes too much to hold "it" anymore. Vanessa's cheeks were stained with tears.

I have thought about that night a lot. The theme song to these memories is a cross between Ice Cube's infectious "It Was a Good Day" chorus because that day certainly was, and a little of the Fresh Prince's "summer, summer, summertime" engulfing cheerfulness. I think about the moments, the "are you going to write about . . . ?" questions, the money manicure, women of their word, the laughter, and the tears. In fact, it is Vanessa's wet cheeks that have made the most lasting impression. Thinking back, I'm not so sure anymore if those tears were from the laughing since ghetto is worth crying over.

. . .

My daughter was three weeks old when I took her to the movies for the first time. It was Wednesday and my ghetto-self would not let some traditions die. My husband and I had hoped to get to the theater in the afternoon so we wouldn't be keeping our little one out too late for our jump-in fix. We discovered, though, that there is no quick exit with children: with the diapers, bottles — "Did I forget anything?" — wipes, blankets, extra onesies — "Did I forget anything?" — and the tears, getting out the door is one long, drawn-out ordeal. By the time we managed to leave the house, it was dark. We were firmly caught in the after-work full-theater crowd heading to an 8 p.m. movie. The mother in me, as new as it was, reluctantly would not allow my ghetto side to indulge in the jump-in and keep my newborn out that late. So we settled for watching only the one movie we actually paid for! In case we would have to make a quick scream-induced exit, we sat in a row by the door with my daughter bundled up in the car seat that we placed on top of an empty seat, rather than on the popcorn-littered floor. Uneventfully, she pretty much slept through the two hours.

"I can't believe you brought a baby to the movies!!!" my friend John tsk-tsked. "I have never heard of that."

"You don't live in Brooklyn!" I shot back with a little too much ghetto pride.

True, we weren't the only ones with children too young at the theater that night. The line for the R-rated shows, which wouldn't be letting out until 10 p.m. or 11 p.m., snaked out the door because of all the strollers. Still, after all those months on the corner, writing about parenting, and responsibilities, and wagging my finger at "Why we gotta be like that?" moments, it was the first time I felt like a hypocrite. In my defense, I explained to John, on that Wednesday night we limited our movie to the PG flick *The Chronicles of Narnia*, based on C. S. Lewis's *The Lion, the Witch, and the Wardrobe*. It was also the first time in years that we had gone to the movies without a jump-in. In the light of John's stare, though, I couldn't even convince myself that my actions weren't ghetto.

The birth of my daughter reminded me that there are no absolutes. Ghetto is a mind-set and we are all infected. But as the Wednesdays increasingly pass by without even an attempted trip to the movies again because taking care of baby comes first, she also constantly reminds me that we can never stop trying to compassionately raise our expectations.

I wipe away my tears from this journey. I am ghetto. I am not ghetto. I am you.

AFTERWORD
FINAL DISPATCH: LIFE SINCE *GHETTONATION*

When my publisher asked me to write some fresh words for the paperback edition of *Ghettonation*, I said yes before my mind had any hint of what I hoped to say with those words. All I knew was that the conversation about ghetto had not ended yet, not even close. In the year since *Ghettonation* originally hit bookshelves I have been invited across the country and back again by those eager for me to talk. More important, judging from the e-mails I continue to get from readers, friends of readers, and those who promise they will become readers once they get the time, you are eagerly talking too. The messages that I cherish the most have come from young people, because their impassioned words continue to give me hope. Overall, this is the conversation that I hoped we would have.

Media interest forced my reporter bones to try to get used to being the one answering the questions instead of asking them. Perhaps proof of just how many lines the ghetto mind-set crosses—from race to class to gender to generation—I have found myself answering questions from a strange mix of company ranging from BET to Bill O'Reilly. No joke. Some people accused me of conservative rhetoric, while others applauded my liberal compassion; some Black folks saw me as a raised-fist-power-to-the-people soldier, while others said they saw a blaming-my-people sellout. The difficulty that people were having trying to find the right box to shove me in reinforced for me how rarely we get to hear the minds of Black women in the national dialogue. Truth is, if Black women were more of a presence in the news as pundits and experts and columnists and talking heads on the Sunday round tables, then my Black woman voice would not have been so hard to identify.

In other news, a few weeks after *Ghettonation*'s release, Rutgers University's Scarlet Knights just missed capturing the NCAA title for women's basketball. And radio host Don Imus opened his mouth and degraded Black women . . . again. The only difference this time around was that America actually noticed. The national dialogue quickly moved from what one white man said to what all Black rappers say. In the tradition of the N-word, *ho* became the new dirty word that everyone couldn't stop saying. Imus lost his job. And Russell Simmons, after first defending hip-hop's use of any and all words during a *ho* discussion on *Oprah*, like any good businessman, responded to market outrage and quickly took back his support and instead ordered a mass mouth washing by calling for hip-hop's ban of the use of the words *ho*, *bitch*, and *nigger*. Moving ahead, Atlanta Falcons quaterback Michael Vick proved just how ghetto he is when he jeopardized his NFL career by funding a dog fighting ring. For the record, contrary to those who tried to excuse his behavior, dog fighting is not a Black "thang"—it is a ghetto "thang." The BET Hip Hop Awards top nominee rapper T.I.—who was nominated for nine awards—was arrested just hours before he was to appear on the show in a federal sting prompted after he allegedly tried to illegally buy three machine guns. His album, "T.I. vs. T.I.P." went on to win CD of the Year at the awards show later that day. O.J. Simpson was charged with armed robbery and kidnapping as a result of a plan too stupid for words to get some of his sports memorabilia from a hotel room in Vegas. And Imus got a new job.

Ghetto ghetto ghetto. Those were just the lowlights.

By far the most e-mails I get since *Ghettonation* was published are from teachers. Black teachers, white teachers, new teachers, veteran teachers. Those who work in big city public schools, close-knit parochial schools, and moneyed private prep schools, from grade school all the way to college professors. Teachers wanted to tell me what was going on in their classrooms. More than anyone else, our educators needed no convincing at all that ghetto is a mind-set—they saw it in their classrooms everyday. Honestly, such support from those who spend their days with our young people scared me a bit. It made me worry that things were even worse than I thought.

That was drilled home when I spoke at a national conference of teachers and school administrators. The conference was an interesting juxtaposition, because it was held for educators of color who worked in the nation's private independent schools, from prep schools to boarding schools—schools that many of us often assume would be a world away from Boys and Girls High in Bed-Stuy. But that day I was reminded that the reality is they share a mind-set. Before this crowd of a couple hundred strong I found myself challenged during our candid conversation. The audience saw the problem intimately and they were searching for solutions. Standing at the frontlines they had "What do I do!?" questions and wanted practical advice. They wanted to know once and for all how to solve this hot ghetto-mess. We all want to know.

That day we talked a lot about the need for a foundation of high expectations and self-respect. People nodded in support. But I was left unsatisfied. I realized in the days and months afterward, as I could not shake the "What do I do" pleas, that perhaps the trouble was that solutions are not just one-step. Instead, the first step is for people to recognize there is a problem. I tried to do that by writing this book. I was starting from a point where I felt people had become too used to the mind-set that was crippling us. The second step is to convince people that the problem affects them directly—that this is not someone else's problem but our problem. Otherwise there will be no legitimate effort to try and find a solution. Only after steps one and two are honestly complete can you move to the "What do I do" step. The "What do I do" step has to be personalized for every situation because a one-brush method rarely works. And there will be stops and starts and changes along the way. Because when you are talking about truly altering behavior and shifting a mind-set, you have to work on the roots first to ensure that a healthier mind will flourish.

The outpouring from teachers made me realize that they are well beyond step one and possibly step two. However, I fear, they are not in the majority. There are still many more among us who have not realized step one yet. I'd say the challenge for those of us who have already taken this step is to open other peoples' eyes to the problem instead of assuming they already see. Unfortunately, they often don't. And seeing there is a problem is part of the solution.

A month before I sat down to write this Afterword, I found in my mailbox amid the bills, junk mail, bills, magazines, and bills something I barely recognized: a personal letter. Fingering the edge of the smaller handwritten envelope I realized I had not received such a relic in more than a decade. My letter was from a high school junior in Frankfort, Illinois, whose school assignment actually was to write and send a letter. The teenager was part of an American civics class and the students were challenged to send their letters to someone they thought was a good citizen. This student's high expectations of me challenged me to consider my own thoughts of what it meant to be a good citizen. A good citizen not simply of a nation but a good citizen of the communities—from neighborhood communities, to family ones, to race or gender or ethnic or spiritual communities, to professional communities, to communities of common interests, etc—all the communities that each of us claims membership to that together build our personal worlds and ultimately our collective nation. With that in mind I wrote back that I thought "our job as good citizens is never to be passive in life. Good citizens are actively involved in creating a better world that is larger than themselves." In other words, the antithesis of ghetto, the devastating mind-set that has taken hold of our nation. Maybe this is the foundation of step two. It's a start. And step three will come.

Lastly, one issue that has come up repeatedly this past year is my use of the word *ghetto* to describe this mind-set of embracing the worst. Some rightfully take issue with painting such a wide canvas of negativity with a word that is so intertwined with poor people of color. Most interesting, many of those who took biggest issue with my use of the word *ghetto* often had little connection or interaction with our young generation. In one case a woman at a discussion in the Bronx admitted that while reading *Ghettonation* she was angered by my use of the word until she discovered afterward how frequently her teenage niece used the word with friends. This auntie still didn't agree with my labeling of this mind-set as ghetto, but she now got where the label came from. I have to admit that I was glad some of us have gotten upset at the free use of the word *ghetto*. As I wrote in the first pages of the Introduction to *Ghettonation*, the race and class connotations of the word can and should never be forgotten. That said, as a journalist I was exposing a window of reality and did not see it as my role to change that view. The word is common vernacular in more circles than some of us care to admit. But, more important to me are the behaviors that inspire the word to be used. Truth is, it is hard to put your finger on exactly what it is to be ghetto. The definition becomes broad and hard to confine. Today a generation is calling it ghetto, tomorrow such self-destructive behavior will be called something else. Because this mind-set crosses race, class, gender, and generational lines equally, I agree a new label would indeed be welcomed. But, I also believe even more strongly that we shouldn't waste time on naming such behaviors and instead focus our energies on the mind-set behind such behaviors. Let's get angry over that! Honestly, the goal, after all, should be to get to the point where the *mind-set* has been virtually wiped out enough that there is no need to label something that is so rarely seen.

This is probably my last Ghettonation dispatch. Thank you for the journey.

Cora Daniels
Brooklyn, NY
January 1, 2008

ENDNOTES

INTRODUCTION

1   *Merriam-Webster's Online Dictionary.*

2   This brief history lesson of ghetto has been compiled by a number of
    sources including Wikipedia: the free encyclopedia; *The Encyclopedia
    of the Holocaust* (Macmillian Publishing Group, 1990); www.death-
    camps.org; Hulda Liberanone "Where Jewish Life Once Thrived," *The
    Jerusalem Report*, June 27, 2005, p. 36; Elyn Aviva, "Life Ever Difficult—
    Paradoxes of the Venetian Ghetto. The Jewish Ghettos in Venice, Italy,"
    World and I, September 1, 2001, p. 180.

3   Christopher Dickey, "The Fire This Time: Years of Racism and Neglect
    Explode in a Week of Riots across France's Mostly Muslim Immigrant
    Ghettos," *Newsweek*, November 14, 2005, p. 16.

4   *The N-Word*, Trio TV original documentary, July 4, 2004. Written and
    directed by Todd Williams, produced by Nelson George.

PROLOGUE

1   Corey Kilgannan, "The Endless Night," *New York Times*, August 21,
    2005, Style section, p. 1.

CHAPTER 1

1   "Iraq: On Whose Behalf? Human Rights and the Economic Reconstruc-
     tion Process in Iraq," Amnesty International, June 20, 2003, MDE
     14/128/2003.

2   Sara Clemence, "Most Expensive Zip Codes 2005 List," Forbes.com and
     U.S. Census Data.

3   Michael Endelman, "Three Days in Crunk Factory, Liquor! Groupies!
     The Singer from Korn! Our Impressionable Young Reporter Barely Sur-
     vives a Weekend in Hip-hop star LIL JON's Miami Mansion," *Entertain-
     ment Weekly*, September 24, 2004, p. 68.

4   Tamar Lewin, "For More People in 20's and 30's, Home Is Where the
     Parents Are," *New York Times*, December 22, 2003, p. B1.

5   Ibid.

6   *Webster's New World College Dictionary*. Editor Michael E. Ayres (John
     Wiley & Sons, 2004).

CHAPTER 2

1   Jeffrey Stanton, "Coney Island—Nickel Empire (1920's–1930's)," 1997,
     North America Integration and Development Center, UCLA.

2   Diane Cardwell, "The Life and Death of a Hip-Hop Jester: Joy, Fame
     and Endless Struggle," *New York Times*, November 18, 2004, p. B1.

3   *The N-Word*, Trio TV original documentary, July 4, 2004. Written and
     directed by Todd Williams, produced by Nelson George.

4   http://www.contribute2.org/. This is David Sylvester's Web site devoted
     to his scholarship bike ride trip across Africa. The "nigger e-mail" is his
     story about the Niggers store. It has been forwarded so many times that
     the story has generated more than six hundred responses from people
     around the world, appeared on Black news sites across the Internet, and
     been mentioned in the mainstream press.

5   Stephen A. Crockett Jr., "Gizoogle.com, the Wizard of Izzle Web Site
     Parody Puts Ya Search Resultizzle into Gansta-speak," *Washington Post*,
     March 10, 2005, p. C1.

6   www.ripodb.tk.

7   Associated Press, "Gwyneth Paltrow Stays Close to Baby Apple at Premiere," September 15, 2005.

8   David Hinckley, "Cutoff Point: The History of Rap in the City," *New York Daily News*, December 8, 2004, p. 35.

9   Erik Parker, "Hip-Hop Goes Commercial," *Village Voice*, September 11–17, 2002, p. 40.

10   Glenn Gamboa, "30 Years of Hip-Hop; Believe the Hype: This Genre's Here to Stay with an Influence beyond Music and into Culture Everywhere," *Newsday*, October 10, 2004, p. A6.

11   "Taking Sexism and Misogyny out of Hip-hop Music," *Talk of the Nation*, host Joe Palca, NPR, February 10, 2005.

12   Kimberly L. Allers, "The New Hustle," *Essence*, August 2005, p. 148.

13   Ibid.

14   Associated Press, "Former BET Host Blasts Videos on Own Show," April 2, 2006.

15   Linton Weeks, "New Books in the Hood; Street Lit Makes Inroads with Readers and Publishers," *Washington Post*, July 31, 2004, p. C1.

16   Gwendolyn Osborne, "The Legacy of Ghetto Pulp Fiction," *Black Issues Book Review*, October 31, 2001, p. 50.

17   Lola Ogunnaike, "For the Novelist Donald Goines, Dead 30 Years, New Popularity and a Movie," *New York Times*, March 25, 2004, p. E1.

18   Dinitia Smith, "Unorthodox Publisher Animates Hip-Hop Lit," *New York Times*, September 8, 2004, p. E6.

19   Malcolm Venable, Tayannah McQuillar, Yvette Mingo, "It's Urban, It's Real, But Is This Literature?; Controversy Rages over a New Genre Whose Sales Are Headed Off the Charts," *Black Issues Book Review*, October 31, 2004, p. 24.

20   "Taking Sexism and Misogyny out of Hip-hop Music," *Talk of the Nation*, host Joe Palca, NPR, February 10, 2005.

21   Lola Ogunnaike, "He Toils, He Spins (on Daytime TV), He Makes 'Ellen' Boogie," *New York Times*, February 7, 2005, p. E1.

22   Ryan Pearson, "Will Smith Wants Rappers to Recognize They're Role
      Models," Associated Press, June 27, 2005.

CHAPTER 3

1   Rachel Morris, "The Shooting." *Columbia Journalism Review*, Septem-
      ber/October 2004, p. 35.
2   Ibid.
3   Ron Howell, "Killing of Timothy Stansbury Jr.: Of Prayers and Protest,"
      New York Newsday, May 16, 2004, p. A6.
4   Michael Brick, "As Furor Dies Down, Teenager's Family Is Left to Suf-
      fer in Private," *New York Times*, April 18, 2004, p. B25.
5   Cheryl L. Reed, "The Fragile Black Middle Class: Race and Money in
      Chicago: Upscale Blacks Drive Prices Up, Forcing Longtime Residents
      Out," *Chicago Sun-Times*, November 14, 2005, p. 12.
6   Ibid.

CHAPTER 4

1   Record Industry Association of America.
2   Gina. M. Wingood, ScD, MPH; Ralph J. Di Clemente, PhD; Jay M.
      Bernhardt, PhD, MPH; Kathy Harrington, MPH, MAEd; Susan L.
      Davis, PhD Med; Alyssa Robilliand, PhD; and Edward W. Hook III,
      MD. "A Prospective Study of Exposure to Rap Music Videos and
      African American Female Adolescents' Health," *American Journal of
      Public Health*, March 2003.
3   Evening broadcast, ABC-7 Chicago, June 18, 2005.
4   Chauncy Baily, "Report Says Oakland Pimps Get Younger," *Oakland
      Tribune*, January 26, 2004.
5   Jeannette De Wyze, "Hooked," *San Diego Magazine*, June 2004.
6   *Scarborough Country*, January 27, 2005, MSNBC.
7   Baily, "Report Says Oakland Pimps Get Younger."
8   www.brandsonsale.com.

9   Gallup Youth Survey, May 24, 2005, Julie Ray, "Adolescents Not Invulnerable to Abusive Relationships."

10 Dr. Edward Laumann, "The Sexual Organization of the City," Chicago Health and Life Survey, University of Chicago, January 8, 2004.

11 Larry E. Davis, "A Black History Month Valentine," *Pittsburgh Post-Gazette*, February 8, 2004, p. E1.

12 Kathleen Kelleher, "Birds and Bees; When It Comes to Love, One Doesn't Seem to Be Enough," *Los Angeles Times*, May 7, 2001, View Desk, p. 2.

13 David P. Barash, PhD, Judith Eve Lipton, MD, *The Myth of Monogamy: Fidelity and Infidelity in Animals and People* (New York: W. H. Freeman, 2001).

14 Marcia Carlson, Sara McLanahan, Paula England, and Barbara Devaney, "What We Know About Unmarried Parents: Implications for Building Strong Families Programs," *Mathematica Police Research in Brief*, January 2005.

15 Sarah McLanahan and Christina Paxson, Fragile Families and Child Wellbeing Study 2005, Princeton University, Irwin Garfinkel, Jeanne Brooks-Gunn, Columbia University; www.fragilefamilies.princeton.edu

16 Ibid.; also Sara McLanahan, "Diverging Destinies: How Children Are Faring under the Second Demographic Transition," *Demography* 41, no. 4 (2004): 607–27; also Marcia Carlson, Sara McLanahan, and Paula England, "Union Formation in Fragile Families," *Demography* 41, no. 2 (2004): 237–61.

17 Kimberly L. Allers, "Real Love," *Essence*, November 2005, p. 191

CHAPTER 5

1   Cornel West, *Race Matters* (Boston: Beacon Press, 1993).

2   Ellis Cose, "Long after the Alarm Went Off," *Newsweek*, March 15, 2005, p. 37.

3   Craig S. Smith, "Magazine's Disclosure Clouds the Future of Monaco's

Royal Line," *New York Times*, May 5, 2005, p. A3; and Craig S. Smith, "The New Prince of Monaco, 47, Confronts His Past as a Playboy," *New York Times*, September 10, 2005, p. A1.

4 Andy Newman and Patrick O'Gilfoil Healy, "Guard Is Burned to Death in Elevator, Two Boys Are Charged," *New York Times*, December 27, 2004, p. B1.

5 Randal C. Archibold and Stacy Albin, "Mother Defends Son, 13, in Prank Turned Fatal Fire," *New York Times*, December 28, 2004, p. B3.

6 Ibid.

7 Nancy Gibbs, "Parents Behaving Badly; Inside the New Classroom Power Struggle: What Teachers Say about Pushy Moms and Dads Who Drive Them Crazy," *Time*, February 21, 2005, cover story.

8 Ibid.

9 Ibid.

10 Ellis Cose, "Long after the Alarm Went Off," *Newsweek*, March 15, 2005, p. 37.

CHAPTER 7

1 Graduation rates are a political issue. The official graduation rate of NYC public schools was 53.2 percent in 2005 according to the mayor's office. Opponents argue that the figure is inflated because it does not consider students who were discharged—those who disappear from the rolls, take longer to graduate, or are pushed out—or special education students who tend never to receive degrees. In 2004 there were 15,626 discharged students from the NYC public school system. When these students are included, the graduation rate is closer to 43.7 percent. For a concise, easy explanation, see Winnie Hu, "Truth Test: Is High School Graduation Rate Up or Down?" *New York Times*, October 12, 2005, p. B4.

2 Interview with Shockwave, *Defend Queens*, October 1, 2002.

3 Don Terry, "A Gang Gives a Name to Students' Fear: Decepticons," *New York Times*, March 1, 1989, p. B1.

4   John Immerwahr, "Public Attitudes on Higher Education: A Trend Analysis, 1993 to 2003." Public Agenda for the National Center for Public Policy and Higher Education, February 2004, and John Immerwahr, "Great Expectations: How the Public and Parents—White, African American, and Hispanic—View Higher Education." Public Agenda for the National Center for Public Policy and Higher Education, 2000.

5   EPIC MRA survey: "Michigan Parents—Culture of Education and Your Child," April 1–21, 2005; and Francis X. Donnelly and Marisa Schultz, "Parents Fail to Push for Education; Poll Shows Hurdles for State's Effort to Shift Economy's Focus from Brawn to Brains," Detroit News, Sunday, May 1, 2005, p. 1A.

6   Felicia R. Lee, "Why Are Black Students Lagging?" New York Times, November 30, 2002, p. B9.

7   Statement by the National Urban League regarding "Black American Students in an Affluent Suburb: A Study of Academic Disengagement," December 4. 2002.

8   Orfield, G., Losen, D., Wald, J., and Swanson, C., Losing Our Future: How Minority Youth Are Being Left Behind by the Graduation Rate Crisis. Cambridge, MA: Civil Rights Project at Harvard University, 2004. Contributors: Advocates for Children of New York, the Civil Society Institute.

9   Advocates for Children of New York.

10 Orfield, G., Losen, D., Wald, J., and Swanson, C., Losing Our Future: How Minority Youth Are Being Left Behind by the Graduation Rate Crisis. Cambridge, MA: Civil Rights Project at Harvard University, 2004. Contributors: Advocates for Children of New York, the Civil Society Institute.

11 David M. Herszenhorn, "Brooklyn High School Is Accused Anew of Forcing Students Out," New York Times, October 12, 2005, p B1.

12 National Governors Association, Summary of RateYourFuture survey findings, July 16, 2005. (The Power Point presentation is available on the NGA Web site as part of "Redesigning the American High School Initiative).

13 SMR Research.

14 American Society of Bariatric Surgery.

15 Marilyn B. Benoit, MD, "The Dot Com Kids and the Demise of Frustration Tolerance" (Study for Campaign for America's Kids, sponsored by the American Academy of Child and Adolescent Psychiatry.)

16 Patrick Welsh, "When the Street and the Classroom Collide," *Washington Post*, Sunday, June 20, 2004, p. B1.

17 Ibid.

18 Ibid.

19 Ibid.

20 "Black Men in Crisis," guests Ronald B. Mincy and Orlando Patterson, *Open Source Radio* with Christopher Lydon, WGBH Boston, March 27, 2006.

21 Orlando Patterson, "A Poverty of the Mind," *New York Times*, Sunday March 26, 2006, Op-Ed page.

22 Orlando Patterson, guest, discussing his *NYT* piece "A Poverty of the Mind," *Talk of the Nation*, the "Op-Ed Pages," March 27, 2006.

23 "Black Men in Crisis," *Open Source Radio*.

24 Patterson, "A Poverty of the Mind."

25 Daniel McGinn, "Mating Behavior 101: Social Scientists Have Recently Begun to Study Sex on Campus, in Search of the Truth about 'Hooking Up,' " *Newsweek*, October 4, 2005.

26 Janny Scott and David Leonhardt, Class Matters Series, "Class in America: Shadowy Lines That Still Divide," *New York Times*, May 15, 2005, p. A1.

CHAPTER 8

1 Transcript of Bill Cosby's speech, NAACP Fiftieth Anniversary *Brown vs. Board of Education* Gala, May 17, 2004, Constitution Hall, Washington, D.C.

2 Ibid.

3 Selwyn Crawford, "Cosby's Criticisms Divide Generations; While Older

Blacks Agree with Him, Youths Say He's Out of Touch," *Dallas Morning News*, October 23, 2004, p. 1A.

4   Scott Fallon, "Moving Up, Staying Up; STRIVE Shows the Down and Out How to Keep a Job," *Bergen Record*, October 26, 2003, p. L1.

5   Tanya Mohn, "Sometimes the Right Approach Is Putting the Best Face Forward," *New York Times*, May 7, 2006, section 10, p. 1.

6   Samantha Marshall, " 'Game Face' Provokes Frowns in Job Market," *Crain's New York Business*, April 11, 2005, p. 11.

7   Transcript of Bill Cosby's speech, NAACP Fiftieth Anniversary *Brown vs. Board of Education* Gala.

8   U.S. Department of Health and Human Services, Administration on Children, Youth and Families, "Child Maltreatment 2004" (Washington, D.C.: U.S. Government Printing Office, 2006).

9   Administration for Children and Families, State Status Series, Definitions of Child Abuse and Neglect, National Clearinghouse on Child Abuse and Neglect Information, 2005.

10 *Nigger: An Autobiography of Dick Gregory*, with Robert Lypstie (New York: E. P. Dutton, Pocket Cardinal Edition, 1964).

11 Sylvester Brown Jr., "Dick Gregory Sheds Light on Cosby's Comments on Race," *St. Louis Post-Dispatch*, May 27, 2004, p. C1.

12 Transcript of Bill Cosby's speech, NAACP Fiftieth Anniversary *Brown vs. Board of Education* Gala.

CHAPTER 9

1   Francis Morrone, *An Architectural Guidebook to Brooklyn* (New York: Gibbs Smith, 2001).

READERS' GUIDE

The issues of *Ghettonation* are ripe for spirited discussion. These questions are meant to inspire critical thinking about the self-destructive mind-set that is crippling American society. If your book club would like to speak to the author, either online or by phone, when it meets to discuss *Ghettonation*, send an e-mail to **info@cora daniels.com** with "book club" in the subject line.

1. What does *ghetto* mean to you?

2. Did your definition change after reading the book? Do you agree with the author's assessment that ghetto is a mind-set? What do you think of her argument that this mind-set crosses race, class, and generational lines?

3. The author included many scenes from her own life as one of the "characters." Although her intention was not to create a memoir, at times the book is very personal. Did you like how she mixed journalism with memoir? Did it add to her argument that we are all in this struggle together?

4. Who or what would you add to the running "That's so ghetto . . ." lists that the author includes in the book? Are there examples the author included that you disagree with?

5. The author's writing style is very conversational and some have

enjoyed the humor. But the book is filled with research, including hundreds of interviews conducted over several years. What anecdote, statistic, or revelation in the book were you most surprised by?

6. Have you ever had a ghetto moment? What is the danger of being numb to ghetto or not seeing ghetto in all its forms?

7. The author's goal was to expose what she feels is a self-destructive mind-set. She calls it "ghetto" because as a journalist that is the word that she found is most commonly used. But given the history of the word *ghetto*, what is the fallout of using the word to describe such a negative mind-set? Does the race of the person using the word make a difference?

8. How is the author's argument different from Bill Cosby's infamous speech at the NAACP dinner?

9. At the end of the book the author concludes that it is time for the ghetto mind-set to "die." Do you agree?

10. The author suggests the first step to wiping out unacceptable behavior that has become acceptable is for each of us to raise our expectations—of ourselves and of others. She has said that is how you gradually raise the bar. Do you think that will help? What is the next step? What can you do in your own community?

© Jamel Toppin

CORA DANIELS is an award-winning journalist whose work has been published in *Fortune*, the *New York Times*, *Essence*, *O: The Oprah Magazine*, *USA Today*, *Heart & Soul*, *FSB: Fortune Small Business*, and *Savoy*. Formerly a veteran *Fortune* writer, she is currently an editor at *Working Mother* and a contributing writer for *Essence*. Daniels has served as a commentator on *ABC News*, CNN, CNBC, BET, NPR, and the *Charlie Rose* show. As an author, she has been called "dynamic," "perceptive," and "a powerful voice from the younger generation." Her first book, *Black Power Inc.*, was dubbed "thought-provoking" by the *Washington Post* and "a must read" by *Black Issues Book Review*. She lives in Brooklyn, New York, with her husband and daughter.